Zavod RAKMO

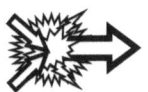

Conflict Competence

Understanding, Assessing and Improving the
Ability to Deal with Conflicts

Marko Iršič

Ljubljana, 2018

Conflict Competence
Understanding, Assessing and Improving the Ability to Deal with Conflicts

Marko Iršič

Edited by Barbar Iršič

Zavod RAKMO, Ljubljana, 2018
1st edition

1.000 copies

Price 19,90 €

info@rakmo.si

www.rakmo.si

© Zavod RAKMO, 2018

CIP - Kataložni zapis o publikaciji
Narodna in univerzitetna knjižnica, Ljubljana

347.919.1
159.913:316.472.42

IRŠIČ, Marko
    Conflict Competence: Understanding, Assessing and Improving the Ability to Deal with Conflicts / Marko Iršič. - 1st ed. - Ljubljana: Zavod Rakmo, 2018

ISBN 978-961-94310-4-7

292812032

To my four sons:
Marko, Jakob, Tadej and Peter with hope
that they will be able to transform the
conflicts they encounter and use them for
progress, personal growth and improvement
of their relationships.

Table of Contents

Introduction 9
Understanding Conflict 11
   What is Conflict 12
      Conflict Interaction 12
      Potential, Latent, Structural and Open Conflict 13
      Types of Incompatibilities 14
      Conflict Expansion and Conflict Escalation 15
      Response to Conflict 16
   Types of Conflict 17
      Focus of Conflict 17
      Visibility of Conflict 17
      Activity of Conflict 17
      Layers of Conflict 18
      Locus of Conflict 19
      The Transformative View of Conflict 20
   Consequences of Unresolved Conflicts 23
   Benefits of (Resolved) Conflicts 25
Conflict Competence 27
   Conflict Sensitivity 29
      Awareness about the Existence of Conflicts 30
      The Ability to Sense and Recognize Conflicts When
      Interaction is Hindered 31
      The Ability to Foresee Conflicts Which May Occur ... 31
      The Ability to Analyze Development and Elements of
      Conflict 32
      The Ability to Consider Different Meanings, Points
      of View, Convictions, Positions and Value Systems 33
      The Ability to Notice Different Understanding or
      Interpretations 33
   Conflict Tolerance 37
      The Ability to Function Despite Conflict 38

    The Ability to Disregard Smaller Conflicts 38
    The Ability to Drop Less Important Issues 39
    The Ability to Understand Smaller Conflicts as Information or Means of Communication 39
    The Ability to Postpone Dealing with an Issue 40
    The Ability to 'Switch' to Another Activity Without Negative Impact of Conflict 41
    The Ability to Ignore Negative Aspects of Interaction 42
    The Ability to 'Switch' to Meta Level of Interaction 43
Influences on Conflict Tolerance 45
    Context 45
    Situation 46
    Psychological State 46
    Physiological State 46
    Transitions 46
    Change 47
    Previously (Un)Resolved Conflicts 47
Assessing Conflict Competence 49
Conflict Competence Questionnaire 50
    Questionnaire: TSC-2017 51
    Calculating the Results 55
    Notes on Copyright and Permission to Use 56
    How to Use the Questionnaire? 57
Ranks of Conflict Competence 59
Types of People in Respect to Conflict Tolerance and Conflict Sensitivity 60
Improving Conflict Competence 61
Improving Conflict Sensitivity 63
    Accepting Conflicts as Part of Reality 64
    (Self)Observation 64
    Analysis of Our Own Conflicts 65
    Analysis of Conflicts We Witness 66
    Analysis of Conflicts in Art, Media and Literature 66
    Learning about Conflicts 67

    Practical and Mental Exercises 67
    Writing Exercises 67
    Strengthening the Ability to Sense, Recognize and Foresee Conflicts 68
    Consciously Considering Different Meanings, Points of View, Convictions, Positions and Value Systems 69
  Raising Conflict Tolerance **71**
    Getting Used to Conflicts 72
    Accepting Responsibility 73
    Leaving Responsibility for Their Actions and Feelings to Others 73
    Understanding Dynamics and Patterns of Conflict 74
    Practicing Conscious Choices in Conflict 75
    Metacommunication, Reflection and Analysis of the Interaction 76
    Consciously Focusing on Current Activity 78
    Consciously Deciding on Importance of Conflicts and Issues 79
    Acquiring and Practicing Skills 79
    Let's do that Again! 80
    Successfully Resolved Conflicts 80
    'Switching out of Conflict' 81
    Consciously Focusing on Constructive Aspects 82
  Managing Conflict Tolerance **84**
    Taking Influences into Account 84
    Changing the Perspective 86
    Broader Context 87
    Preserving or Regaining Internal Stability 87
    Talking to a Friend or Mediator about Conflict 89
    Proposing Mediation or Communication Wellness 89
    Using Mediation or Communication Wellness 90
Conclusion **92**
References **94**
About the Author **99**
About Rakmo Institute **100**

Introduction

There is a wealth of knowledge, research, books and training programs about skills and techniques of conflict resolution and conflict transformation, however despite of the vast amount of it, conflicts in general are dealt with poorly, even more, oftentimes they are not even recognized as such before it is too late.

One of the reasons is that conflicts are for the most part not understood, accepted as part of reality, nor dealt with consciously. Rather than that, people are dealing with conflicts spontaneously, which is in most cases the exact opposite of how they should act.

In addition, people generally perceive the conflict as the other person's fault and themselves as the other's victim or, when refusing to be a victim, a righteous 'punisher'. Since the other person responds in the same way, the conflict only escalates.

There are, however, individuals, groups and sometimes cultures that have a habit of dealing with conflicts productively, namely using a conflict for progress, growth and the improvement of relationships. And they are, knowingly or unknowingly, treating the phenomenon of conflict differently than others.

In general, we can call the characteristic that differentiates people who deal with conflicts productively from the rest, conflict competence. It is not a particular set of skills 'per se', but rather a general approach and attitude towards conflict.

Consequently, rather than offering techniques and guidelines for successful conflict management, this book focuses on understanding, assessing and developing the ability to deal with conflicts, which we call **conflict competence**.

This book is therefore not a handbook for learning the skills, nor does it present an overview of skills or methods for dealing with conflicts constructively. It rather presents a concept of conflict competence as a predisposition for dealing with conflicts productively, proposes and describes a tool for their assessment and gives some general guidelines and suggestions for developing conflict competence.

Understanding Conflict

Conflict is a part of life, an ingredient of human reality. Conflict can bring progress, but it can also undermine functioning. Conflict can bring personal growth, but can also ruin lives. It can develop relationships but also bring them to a bitter end.

The key, however, is not in the existence of conflict, but in the way how individuals, groups and societies deal with it. In order to be able to deal with it appropriately, one has to understand it better.

The concept of conflict is briefly presented and discussed below. This description, however, does not present a thoroughly elaborated presentation and explanation of conflict, but rather a brief overview in order to illustrate the complexity and multi-layeredness of the phenomenon that people know and understand so little.

What is Conflict

There are many different definitions of conflict offered by various authors. One distinction that we can make among various definitions of conflict is whether they define conflict as an interaction (e.g. constructive vs. destructive) or as a state of affairs (e.g. incompatibility of goals).

One general definition that I proposed (Iršič, 2002; Iršič, 2004) is: *Conflict is a situation where two or more systems within a system or a territory function sub-optimally due to their (partial) incompatibility.* Translated to interpersonal relationships that would mean: *Interpersonal conflict is a situation where two or more individuals in a relationship or within a group or in a certain field function sub-optimally due to their (partial) incompatibility.*

Conflict Interaction

Obviously, the definition presented above refers to conflict as a state of affairs but also includes interaction hindered by incompatibility. Referring to incompatibility or conflict, however, there can be explicit or implicit interaction, which we can call conflict interaction.

Obviously, we can distinguish between constructive and destructive conflict interaction, depending on whether the interaction leads to improvement (resolution or transformation, progress, growth, etc.) or it is making things worse.

In the following pages the term conflict will be used in both meanings: conflict interaction and state of affairs, which will be clear from the context, in some cases, however, with the goal of greater clarity, the terms **conflict interaction** or **structural conflict** will be used.

Potential, Latent, Structural and Open Conflict

Conceptually we can distinguish between potential, latent, structural and open conflict.

Potential conflict is actually not a conflict per se, but rather an incompatibility of a sort that can become a source of conflict.

Structural conflict means incompatibility (of goals, values, knowledge, habits, etc.) that hinders the optimal functioning of the individual, group/organization or society.

Open conflict means every visible conflict interaction (e.g. a quarrel or ignoring each other), irrespective of whether it is known what causes it or which are the incompatibilities behind it.

Latent conflict, on the other hand, refers to a structural conflict that is not yet visible or is at the moment not causing difficulties because there is, for example, no interaction or activity related to it.

If there is no interaction related to the incompatibility at the moment, but the incompatibility that exists is responsible for suboptimal functioning, we can talk about *latent conflict*; if, on the other hand, a certain incompatibility (e.g. religion, political convictions etc.) does not contribute to suboptimal functioning or cooperation at all, then we can understand it merely as a *potential conflict*. The term potential conflict therefore refers only to areas in which individuals (or systems) in general do not interact.

Types of Incompatibilities

Incompatibilities that can be a source of conflicts are numerous. The incompatibility which is the most commonly referred to as a source of conflict is the incompatibility of goals. However, in addition, there can be a vast amount of other incompatibilities responsible for conflict that we may not even be aware of, for example incompatible perceptions of the situation, incompatible meanings of words or incompatible expectations, to name just a few. In the table below, there is an incomplete list of possible incompatibilities to illustrate the variety of incompatibilities that can lead to conflict.

Information	Values	Importance of relationship
Knowledge	Beliefs	
Meanings of a word or concept	Ways of functioning	Perceptions of the situation
Intent of statement or message	Habits	Understanding of agreement
	Personalities	
	Attention	Importance of agreement
Goals	Emotions	
Interests	Feelings	Responses to conflict
Positions	Energy levels	
Viewpoints	Motivation	Conflict tolerance
Whishes	Rhythms	
Wants	Procedures	Perception of conflict, etc.
Needs	Responsibilities	
Expectations	Social roles	
Convictions	Attitudes towards others	
Perceptions		

Table 1: Various incompatibilities as possible sources of conflicts

Obviously, there can be incompatibilities such as listed above between individuals or groups, but there could be incompatibilities within an individual or a group as well.

In most cases, there are several or even numerous incompatibilities responsible for conflict, out of which most are not even consciously noticed. In addition, they are interconnected, so conflict interaction oftentimes quickly spreads and escalates.

Conflict Expansion and Conflict Escalation

Irrespective of the incompatibilities involved, conflict interaction has a tendency to expand (conflict expansion) and escalate (conflict escalation). In general, conflict expansion refers to the increase in topics or issues involved, and conflict escalation refers to the intensity of conflict interaction (emotions, volume, speed, etc.)

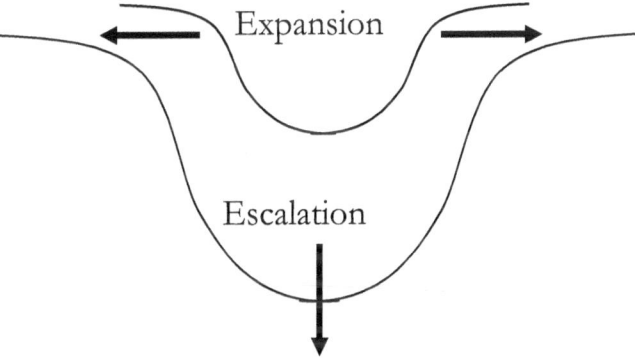

Figure 1: Conflict expansion and conflict escalation (Iršič, 2010)

Response to Conflict

There are many different responses and classifications of responses to conflict but in general we can distinguish between avoidance (withdrawing, changing the subject, not responding, etc.) and engagement (compromise, collaboration, competition, etc.).

Obviously, both refer to conflict interaction which can be constructive or destructive, and not to conflict as such. One can, for example, not avoid conflict if it exists, but can avoid talking about it or engaging in a quarrel over the incompatibility concerned.

To elaborate on the issue a bit more, we can distinguish between five mayor types of response, namely: avoidance, accommodation, compromise, competition and collaboration, which can be either spontaneous or automatic or consciously chosen, depending on the importance of our own interest and the importance of the relationship or the other's interest.

If both are important, collaboration is the most suitable response. If neither is important, avoidance may be appropriate. And if both are partially important, then compromise might do the job. On the other hand, if our interest is very important and the relationship is not, then competition or imposing our own outcome might be in place, but if the relationship and/or the interest of the other is very important, whereas our interest is not, then accommodation may be a better option.

Types of Conflict

Taking into account the variety and amount of possible incompatibilities, out of which many may not even be conscious, we can, with respect to the manifestation of conflict, distinguish between different types, irrespective of the specific incompatibilities involved.

Focus of Conflict

The focus of the conflict can be an **issue**, a **person** or a **relationship** related to first, second and third degree of conflicts which involve progressively more destructive tactics (Rausch et al., 1974). When conflicts are issue focused, the stress tends to be placed on defeating the problem, not the other person and such conflicts are much more likely to be successfully resolved. On the other hand, if conflicts are focused on a person or relationship, they tend to be more difficult. Parties in conflict can to a certain degree choose how to see conflict in terms of what they focus on, or how they frame the issues and consequently influence the difficulty of their conflict.

Visibility of Conflict

With respect to the visibility, we can differentiate between **suppressed**, **covered** and **open** conflicts. A suppressed conflict is the one that we are not aware of, but it impacts our functioning nevertheless. A covered conflict is the one that we know about, but we act as if it did not exist, possibly we also avoid the interaction related to it. An open conflict is the one that is noticed and people are aware of it, but this does not mean that they deal with it constructively.

Activity of Conflict

Conflict can be **active** or **passive**. A passive conflict is the one that does not change, does not spread, is not being resolved nor dealt with in any way. An active conflict, on the other hand, is the one that changes positively or negatively (e.g. escalates, expands, is being resolved or transformed, etc.)

Background of Conflict

With respect to the background, we can distinguish between independent, consequential, transferred and artificially created conflicts. **Independent conflict** means that it stems from incompatibility that we deal with. **Consequential conflict** means that it stems from a deeper incompatibility (e.g. incompatibility of goals stems from incompatibility of values). And **transferred conflict** is the one that originates in other conflicts (oftentimes those that we are not aware of or those we cover) even if it is not directly related to them (for example, since I dislike the other person I support the idea given by someone else). Conflict can also be **artificially created**, for example, when someone does not want to fulfill a promise and gets involved in a conflict over something else with the other and consequently has an excuse for revoking the promise or causing the other to not wanting to ask for its fulfillment. The distinction between artificially created and transferred or consequential conflict is, however, not very clear.

Layers of Conflict

With respect to the 'depth' of conflict, we can differentiate between dispute, underlying conflict, deep-rooted conflict and legacy-based conflict (Ridgewood Foundation, 2002). **Dispute** is in general a disagreement about the content the parties are discussing and presents incompatibility on the surface. More often than not, there is an **underlying conflict** related to the dispute in question. If that is not the case, the disputes are fairly easily resolved or settled. Underlying conflict refers to issues that are not necessarily openly discussed (e.g. feelings, respect, relationship, needs, etc.)

Even deeper and more complex than that is a **deep-rooted conflict** that is related to generalized beliefs and may be based on stereotypes and prejudices. It is complex, interwoven and usually under the surface. Its existence often secures and nourishes further conflict.

Legacy-based conflict is the accumulation and 'ferment' of all disputes, underlying and deep-rooted conflicts together with the trauma, drama alienation and chaos of the fundamental conflict.

Locus of Conflict

In terms of locus, one can differentiate between intrapersonal and interpersonal, as well as intra group and intergroup conflict where individuals and groups can be interdependent or independent entities (Combs & Avrunin, 1989).

Internal or **intrapersonal** conflict refers to conflict within the individual and **can be due to any incompatibility of the individual** (e.g. values and motivation, loyalty and righteousness, goals and energy level, etc.) **including the desire that the reality would be different than it is.**

Conflict **between individuals or groups** that are **interdependent** means that the outcome of conflict has a direct impact on both/all sides, and conflict between **independent entities** refers to a situation where decisions and actions are and can be made by each side autonomously, but are not necessarily approved by the other side/s and consequently they respond unilaterally as well. Even if parties are autonomous, there are nevertheless interests or other aspects that are interwoven, otherwise there would be no conflict among them. The distinction between the second and the third type is not very clear, as the question of autonomy is relative and in addition it can change by separation or merger (consensual/voluntary or forced).

Furthermore, the distinction between internal and external conflict is not perfectly clear since internal conflict can induce external conflict, or one side can 'push' one part of the internal conflict to the other. In addition, external conflict also induces internal conflict or can even be 'absorbed' by one side in order to prevent further damage, which is in most cases done sub- or semiconsciously. Furthermore, internal conflict of one side can also induce internal conflict in the other side and vice versa.

Grammar of Conflict

In every lasting relationship there develop stable patterns of interaction. Some of them, however, might be dysfunctional and responsible for reoccurring conflicts. It is known that in stressful situations only well-rehearsed behaviors are available, the more so the higher the stress. Therefore, even though one or both participants involved in the conflict subsequently regret it and apologize to each other, it is likely that it will reoccur. Even if the issue was subsequently resolved, the same type of conflict interaction will most likely occur again with a different issue. That is what we call 'grammar of conflict', the same grammar with a different content.

Similarly, as in relationships, grammar of conflict exists also in society in general and is for the most part not consciously noticed or understood. It differs to a lesser or bigger degree from culture to culture, but within a culture it is fairly consistent. Consequently, even people who have never seen each other before can engage in similar types of interaction following the same patterns or grammar of conflict.

The Transformative View of Conflict

According to the transformative view, conflict is a crisis of human interaction. It tends to destabilize parties' experience of self and the other. People in conflict tend to experience relative weakness and self-absorption. These negative dynamics tend to feed into each other in a vicious circle. As a result, the interaction quickly degenerates and assumes a mutually destructive, alienating and dehumanizing character (Bush and Folger, 2005).

However, despite the destabilizing impact of conflict, people have the ability to rebound and recover from its alienating effects. Specifically, people can and indeed do make dynamic shifts along two dimensions while conflict unfolds: empowerment (shifts towards increasing clarity, confidence, personal strength, organization, decisiveness) and recognition (shifts towards increasing attentiveness to the other, responsiveness to the other, openness to the other's humanity and appreciation for the other's situation). Thus, despite the potentially destructive impacts of conflict, people have the capacity to move back into their sense of personal strength or self-confidence (the empowerment shift) and into their sense of openness or responsiveness to the other (the recognition shift). As these positive shifts feed into each other, the interaction can regenerate and assume a constructive, connecting and humanizing character (Bush and Folger, 2005).

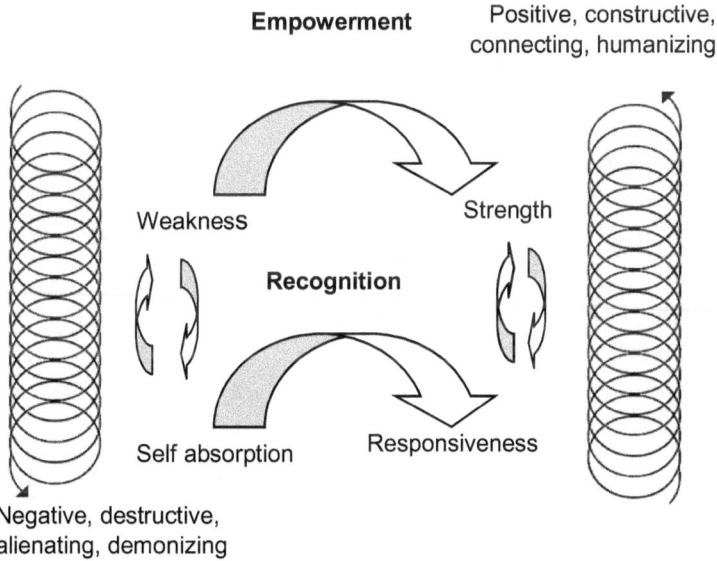

Figure 2: Model of conflict transformation (Bush and Folger, 2005)

State of Strength and State of Weakness

If people interact constructively, they often feel calmer, clearer, more confident, more focused, more decisive, more articulate, etc. (state of strength) and they are also more attentive to the other, more open, more able to see the other's perspective, willing to consider the other's interests and their feelings (responsiveness). If people interact in a state of strength and responsiveness to the other, the outcome of their interaction will most likely be constructive and will bring even more clarity and strength, as well as more willingness to be responsive to the other.

In a destructive conflict, people experience relative weakness and self-absorption. In conflict, we often feel unsettled, confused, fearful, disorganized, unsure, anxious, etc. (state of weakness) and also self-protective, defensive, suspicious, focused on our own interests, thoughts and feelings (self-absorption). If both parties feel that way, their interaction will almost invariably be destructive, which will in turn only contribute to their state of relative weakness and self-absorption within that interaction or that relationship.

But what happens if one party is in a state of strength and responsiveness and the other in a state of weakness and self-absorption? That is an unstable combination which does not last long, and it can go either way, depending on the intensity or stability of the one or the other, unless interaction is ended soon. Oftentimes, the one who is in a state of weakness and self-absorption to a certain extent 'surprises' the other who is maybe in a normal mode of strength and responsiveness, and consequently drags him or her down to a state of weakness and self-absorption as well. On the other hand, if the other party is either prepared or strong enough, he or she can gradually contribute to the first party regaining strength and responsiveness merely by preserving their own state of strength or internal stability and at the same time continuing interaction with the other (Iršič, 2017).

Consequences of Unresolved Conflicts

When conflicts occur and are not resolved or transformed soon, we pay a substantial price, not only in terms of money but also in terms of health (physical and psychological), vitality, motivation, general wellbeing, time, etc.

There are several negative consequences of unresolved conflicts in general, like: lack of good atmosphere, lower quality of communication and deteriorating relationships, disintegration of organization or relationship, stagnation, excommunication, violence, abuse and oppression, psychological disorders, psychosomatic diseases, disruption of optimal interaction, among others (Iršič, 2004).

There are additional negative consequences related to the milieu where conflicts exist, for example, at the workplace: lower work motivation, lack of cooperation, lower productivity, misunderstandings at delegating tasks, higher costs, difficulties in functioning, possible court procedures, termination of work relationships, distrust in co-workers or employees, and others (Iršič, 2010b).

In general, each unresolved conflict creates an obstacle for communication. In every relationship, there are many differences and incompatibilities that do not on their own represent conflict. However, as soon as interaction develops in an area where that discrepancy is relevant, it presents a difficulty in interaction and functioning, and a conflict occurs. If parties successfully resolve or transform conflict, it disappears; on the other hand, if they do not, which means that they or at least one of them is left frustrated, that particular area of interaction is consciously or subconsciously perceived as dangerous or troublesome.

Consequently, parties repeatedly engage in destructive conflict interaction related to that particular area, on the one hand, and try to avoid or bypass it, on the other. Irrespective of their response, either engaging in or avoiding destructive conflict interaction, productive communication in that area is blocked. Since areas of interaction are also related to each other, the conflict gradually spreads.

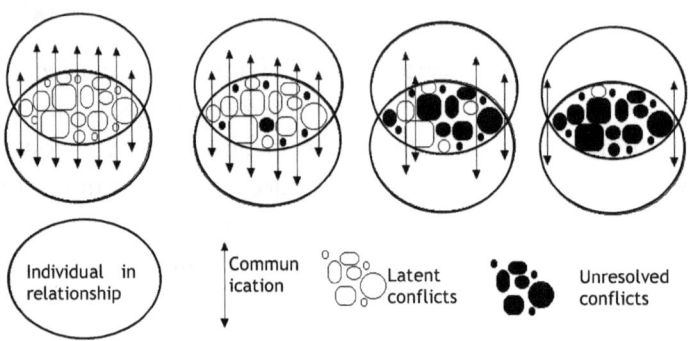

Figure 3: Decrease in the possibility for productive communication between parties as a consequence of unresolved conflicts (Iršič, 2004)

Like demonstrated in Figure 3 each unresolved conflict presents an obstacle for productive communication in the future until it is resolved. Eventually, such unresolved conflicts pile up and with time make it close to impossible to communicate productively with each other. Consequently, destructive interaction is more and more common and eventually (if nothing changes) the relationship is doomed to fail.

Benefits of (Resolved) Conflicts

On the other hand, resolved conflicts bring various benefits, ranging from improved atmosphere, better communication, higher motivation, better relationships, better understanding and even improved health and general wellbeing.

Furthermore, resolved conflicts bring personal growth, higher level of communication culture and quality of cooperation, better understanding of oneself and each other, as well as improved trust towards each other and oneself.

In addition, conflicts are indicators of problems that need to be resolved and mobilize the energy which we can use for that purpose. They foster change and contribute to better decisions. Conflicts also break monotony and decrease tension in everyday interactions.

Conflicts can thus be highly beneficial to individuals, relationships, communities and society in general. The only reason that conflicts do not contribute to all the benefits stated above is the fact that people are not used to using them for this purpose since they do not see conflicts as opportunities, but as threats. Consequently, people tend to avoid conflicts rather than use them for personal growth, progress and improvement of relationships.

Conflict, however, is a situation where we are confronted with something that transcends our current level of maturity, skill, wisdom, understanding and knowledge, and therefore, they somewhat ironically present an opportunity to transcend our limitations, and it is up to us if we use them for this purpose or not.

Conflicts also present the opportunity for constructive interaction (as well as the danger for destructive one) and it is up to us if we are able to take such an opportunity. That however, depends to a large extent on the severity of conflict, on the one hand, and on the level of our conflict competence, on the other.

Conflict Competence

Conflict competence is a characteristic of individuals (and also groups and cultures for that matter) who deal with conflicts constructively, that is to say, they deal with conflicts in such a way that they bring growth rather than destruction, that they improve relationships rather than damage or ruin them and that they bring progress rather than war.

It is not so much about specific techniques they use, but rather about their general approach and demeanor related to conflicts. Conflict competence is an acquired capacity of individuals, groups and cultures to sense and recognize the conflict behind disruption of communication or interaction, and they are able to transform it or able to accept and live with it.

Conflict competence can also be defined as a combination of conflict tolerance and conflict sensitivity (Iršič, 2010).

Conflict competence comprises two elements, namely conflict sensitivity and conflict tolerance, which are presented below. Conflict sensitivity refers to the ability of individuals to sense and recognize a conflict in interactions or relationships and conflict tolerance refers to the ability to function constructively even if there is conflict. The higher conflict tolerance the more conflict one is able to endure and preserve constructive behavior. (Iršič, 2017)

Conflict competence refers to a combination of both, conflict sensitivity and conflict tolerance, that is the ability to recognize conflicts and the ability to preserve constructive functioning in face of conflict. Obviously, the advantages of both are combined and the combination determines specific response to conflict, as well as individual's general style of dealing with conflicts as briefly illustrated in chapter entitled *Types of People with Respect to Conflict Tolerance and Conflict Sensitivity*.

If one is able to recognize conflicts soon enough (a high level of conflict sensitivity) and is able to endure strong conflicts and still preserve constructive functioning (high conflict tolerance), one is more likely to deal with conflicts productively than if either or both of those characteristics are low.

A study conducted by Rakmo Institute in 2016 revealed a correlation between conflict competence and physical health, psychological health and satisfaction at the workplace, as well as satisfaction in the relationship with children (Iršič, 2018).

Conflict Sensitivity

Conflict sensitivity, as mentioned above, refers to the ability of individuals to sense and recognize a conflict in interactions or relationships. Conflict sensitivity includes awareness about the existence of conflicts, the ability (and willingness) to sense and recognize conflicts when interaction is hindered, the ability to foresee conflicts which may occur, the ability to analyze development and elements of conflict, the ability to consider different meanings, points of view, convictions, positions and value systems, and the ability to notice different understanding or interpretations.

Conflict sensitivity also refers to a general ability to assess how optimally the system (a group, an organization, a relationship, etc.) functions and to sense its suboptimal functioning if it exists. It does not mean being "oversensitive" to disruptions or conflict or being distressed or blocked by them. It refers in general to detection and recognition of conflict and not to feeling frustrated or hindered by the conflict.

Awareness of the Existence of Conflicts

A key element of conflict sensitivity is the awareness of the existence of conflicts that are present all around us and accepting them as a normal part of reality. The illusion of harmony is counterproductive and contributes to stress and helplessness when the harmony is disrupted. It also contributes to conflicts being perceived as bad and damaging without having any real tools to deal with them.

The more we are aware of the existence of conflicts and the more we are able to accept them as a normal part of life, the better we are able to notice them sooner rather than later. Obviously, every conflict can eventually lead to danger and even violence or abuse if not dealt with appropriately in time. Therefore, it is important to be able to notice them sooner rather than latter, which is much easier if we are aware of their existence and accept their presence as a normal part of life.

It is also important to be able to distinguish between conflict and abuse or violence (verbal, physical, psychological, social, etc.). Abuse and violence are not conflict, but rather destructive responses to conflict (which obviously create more unproductive conflict) and are largely also a result of not being aware of conflicts and consequently not dealing with them appropriately and soon enough. The distinction between conflict and violence or abuse is crucial because, even if they are many times interwoven in practice (mostly due to lack of awareness and functional skills), they are far from being the same. Whereas conflicts are generally an opportunity for growth, progress and the improvement of relationship and therefore intrinsically good, that is seldom the case with violence and abuse.

Being aware of conflicts, separating them from violence and being able to recognize them at their early stages consequently contribute also to the prevention of violence and abuse and to a higher quality and culture of communication and relationships.

The Ability to Sense and Recognize Conflicts When Interaction is Hindered

Due to a lack of awareness combined with a lack of knowledge and skill on how to deal with conflicts productively, people tend to not only avoid dealing with conflicts but also avoid recognizing them. Denying the existence of conflicts or pretending they do not exist is counterproductive in the long run.

The ability to sense and recognize conflicts does not necessarily mean that we will engage in them or try to sort them out on the spot. It only means that we notice and recognize them and are aware of the fact they exist. Consequently, we can take them into account, deal with them or accommodate them or we can still decide to avoid dealing with them, but at least in that case it is a conscious choice.

Not being able to consciously recognize the existence of conflict prevents us from addressing conflict appropriately, which often results in frustration and blaming the other. The irony is that the other tends to reciprocate such attitude, which only makes matters worse.

The Ability to Foresee Conflicts Which May Occur

Another important aspect of conflict sensitivity is the ability to foresee conflicts which may occur. Not in terms of being afraid of them in advance but to be able to prepare to deal with them appropriately when they come or even to be able to prevent them from happening.

If we notice we are involved in a conflict only after the conflict interaction is already very intense and destructive or already over, it is quite different than if we notice or foresee a potential conflict long before it occurs. We have much more time and options to choose from, and consequently we can deal with it much more constructively.

To use a metaphor, if when driving, we notice a car that is driving towards us only seconds before the potential crash or even after the crash, it is quite different than seeing the approaching car more than hundred meters away.

The Ability to Analyze Development and Elements of Conflict

Being aware of what is happening and what we are doing when conflict occurs is another rarely possessed skill. In most of the cases of destructive conflict interaction, both sides are acting automatically with limited awareness and severely decreased capacity of conscious choices and behavior which they often regret subsequently. That is also one of the reasons that people are afraid of conflicts and try to avoid them.

That, however, does not help. Rather, it would be better if we tried to increase the awareness of what is happening (and not let emotions cloud our perception, understanding and judgment) and reclaim our capacity of conscious decision making even in conflict.

People often regret they did not remain calm or wish they would be able to do so next time. However, it is difficult to remain calm without knowing or understanding what exactly is happening.

Being consciously aware and subsequently being able to analyze what was going on, who said or did what and how did the interaction unfold, contributes to a conscious control over the situation and our responses. Even if we fail to remain calm and practice a conscious choice, at least we are more aware where we failed and what contributed to it, so we can prepare for the next time.

The Ability to Consider Different Meanings, Points of View, Convictions, Positions and Value Systems

Another important skill is the ability to take into account the possibility of different meanings, points of view, convictions, positions and value systems, etc. Even when using the same words, we do not necessarily mean the same things or have the same emotions attached to words. Nor do we all hold the same convictions, beliefs and values. Inability to consider differences in this respect contributes to frustration due to a lack of understanding of what is going on.

If we assess the situation wrongly, we are less likely to choose the appropriate response. Without, for example, understanding that the other understood our words differently, we may be inclined to attribute the results to his/her lack of motivation, incompetence or even malice. On the other hand, if we correctly determine that there was a misunderstanding, we can clarify it and we can adopt measures to make sure that this does not happen next time.

All too often people think that what is evident or clear to them, holds true for the other person as well, and that what they think or believe, is the only correct thing. Therefore, if others hold different views or values or think differently *it must be something wrong with them.*

Being able to, at least temporarily, explore different meanings, values, positions, etc. contributes strongly to the correct assessment of the situation and greater clarity.

The Ability to Notice Different Understanding or Interpretations

In addition to allowing for or taking into account the differences, it is also important to be able to notice them when they take place.

Not only considering them generally, but actually noticing them when they are at work, even if it is not so clear.

We may for example understand that there can be different meanings, interpretations and understanding, but fail to notice them, when they are at work. Consequently, we may proceed with communication or cooperation under the illusion of understanding, only to discover later that something went wrong.

Therefore, noticing the differences in understanding or interpretations early on can save us much unnecessary work, tension or frustration. Obviously, that requires an 'open mind' in terms of allowing for others to think differently than we do, and not only in terms of right and wrong, but in terms of different interpretations which can all make sense, at least from different points of view.

This does not mean that we necessarily treat them as equally good or correct, nor that we have no means of finding out which one is more appropriate, but it does mean that we notice the indications of differences in understanding or interpretations and consequently recognize those differences or check how one or the other understands things, and verify if there is a misunderstanding involved or not.

Many conflicts start as misunderstandings which are not recognized as such in time. As interaction unfolds, however, conflict and its consequences become real and prevent the realization that there was a mere misunderstanding initially involved. It is not very common to double check how things were understood and usually people take it for granted that everyone understands things the same way.

There are many factors however which impact understanding, including the worldview, beliefs, previous experiences, knowledge and information, to name just a few. In addition, there are sometimes slight nuances in understanding which can change the meaning of a message. The context, nonverbal expression and the tone of voice have an impact on the correct understanding of what was said. In addition to words, there are also actions and behavior that are even easier to interpret differently and people do not normally check with the other what was meant, but tend to fill in their own interpretations and understanding.

Therefore, the ability to sense and recognize potential misunderstandings or different interpretations is very useful in this respect, since it is much easier to clarify things at the stage of misunderstanding than to realize, after the destructive actions and behavior and potential consequences already piled up, that initially there was only a misunderstanding.

Conflict Tolerance

Conflict tolerance is the ability to function constructively even if there is conflict. The higher conflict tolerance the more conflict one is able to endure and preserve constructive behavior. The threshold is reached when responses of an individual stop being constructive (e.g. stops listening, starts attacking the other, behaves defensively, bursts out, etc.).

Conflict tolerance includes the ability to: function in spite of conflict; drop less important issues; disregard smaller conflicts; understand smaller conflicts as information or means of communication; postpone dealing with particular issue; 'switch' to another activity without negative impact of conflict; 'switch' to meta level of interaction and the ability to ignore negative aspects of interaction and respond to positive ones when communication includes both.

The Ability to Function Despite Conflict

The ability to function despite conflict is crucial for human existence. If every little conflict blocked our functioning, people would not be able to function at all.

Obviously, there is a huge difference if conflict is major or minor, but in any case, it is important to be able to function nevertheless. Some conflicts are much more difficult to deal with, but the more difficult the conflicts we can endure and still function well, the higher our conflict tolerance.

The ability to function despite conflict, does not mean that we ignore conflict or that we suppress it. It merely means that the existence of conflict does not block us completely.

The Ability to Disregard Minor Conflicts

Furthermore, the ability to disregard minor conflicts is another component of conflict tolerance. Obviously, it does not refer to conflict over important aspects or issues, but to minor ones that need not be resolved and actually do not have a real impact on anything.

Being upset or in a state of weakness over unimportant conflicts undermines our ability to deal constructively with important ones and at the same time drains our energy needed for productive activity or work in general.

Therefore, being able to just disregard or ignore minor conflicts is functional, since it frees up our energy to function and also deal with more important ones appropriately.

It is not so clear, however, what is a minor or less important conflict is, but as a rule of thumb: If we could live a good life without ever resolving that conflict, it probably means that it is not a very important one.

The Ability to Drop Less Important Issues

Similarly, a further element of conflict tolerance is the ability to drop less important issues. The difference lies in whether the discussion over a certain issue already started or not. If we started a discussion over an issue that is not so important, we can also just drop it, either explicitly (e.g. by saying 'Let's drop it.') or implicitly by changing the topic of conversation and never coming back to it.

There are almost infinite number of possible issues or disagreements that one could engage in. However, a lot of them are not important or relevant at all and most of them are not very important. So, one literally does not have enough time to deal with all of them. If the issues are very important, one should obviously not drop them, but one can easily drop most of them. That is not to say that one should drop every issue which is not very important, but it is good if one is able to do so without staying upset if s/he chooses to do so.

It is sometimes not so clear, however, what are important and less important issues, especially since our responses are to a large extent automatic, and ironically, due to intensive responses also to unimportant issues they seem to be important retroactively. To counter that, we can ask ourselves a series of questions, like: Is this important? If so, how much? Why? What are the possible consequences of this one way or the other? What does it mean? Does it really mean that? etc.

The Ability to Understand Minor Conflicts as Information or Means of Communication

Similarly, another component of conflict tolerance is being able to understand minor conflicts as information or means of communication. Some conflicts can be due to suboptimal mode of communication. For example expressing a need or an interest one has, but in a manner that is not necessarily appreciated by the other. It can be due to various reasons either temporary (e.g. headache, tiredness, illness, stress, etc.) or long-term (e.g. not being used to express things politely).

In both cases one can either engage in attempts to improve the quality of communication or one can understand the issue or the need behind the conflict and address it directly rather than get involved in a discussion or conflict over the way it was expressed. One can even articulate it in a more productive way (reframe the statement, that is capture the main message, and formulate it in a more productive manner).

It is important however, that one does not do that from a state of weakness or out of subordination or fear, but from a state of strength, which allows him or her to preserve productive orientation and not suffer the consequences of suppressed conflict, which would occur otherwise.

Obviously, if a certain type of unproductive mode of communication is repeated many times, it is eventually advisable to deal with it and build a more productive or satisfying pattern of interaction. However, that can also happen as a side effect of consistently responding productively to an unproductive formulation of issues, needs or desires.

The Ability to Postpone Dealing with an Issue

Similar to being able to drop less important issues, it is important that one is able to postpone dealing with a particular issue to a more appropriate moment or context. Some issues are important enough not to disregard them and at the same time not such that one can just take them in a positive way, but they call for some transformation or resolution. However, it may be that at the time when they occur, it is not possible or appropriate to deal with them on the spot. In such a case, it is useful if one is able to postpone dealing with them.

One option how to propose to postpone the dealing with the conflict is a phrase "Let's put this into brackets. It can also be used, obviously, to just drop the issues, depending on their importance.

But in any case, it is important to be able to postpone dealing with the issue to more a appropriate moment. Not being able to do so, hinders our general ability to function efficiently or interact with others productively.

An alternative to the statement above is also: "Let's deal with that later." (for example after the meeting, tomorrow morning, in the evening, when the kids are in bed, when we go for a walk, at the next meeting, during lunch break, etc.) It is important to define at least to some extent the time when the issue will be dealt with (unless it is already a common practice to deal with the issues in time), otherwise the proposal to deal with the issue later could be perceived merely as a nicer way of trying to avoid dealing with it altogether. Furthermore, if often occurs that we do not get back to dealing with it, it will not be useful for long.

Sometimes taking a break from a certain discussion ("Let's take a break!") is also very productive, especially if one or both/all parties became upset, so they can calm down and also think about the issues calmly before continuing to deal with them. This also requires the ability to postpone dealing with the issues at least for a short time. When taking a break, it is important to agree on it explicitly (otherwise the other/s might not know what is happening or why one is leaving the discussion) and agree about the length (e.g. 20') and to return to dealing with the issue (similarly to when postponing the discussion) after the break.

The Ability to 'Switch' to Another Activity Without Negative Impact of Conflict

Sometimes it is important that we do some work without a negative impact of the other circumstances, be it with the same person whom we had conflict with or in a different context. Sometimes it is not possible or appropriate to deal with the issues on the spot, but at the same time we have not been able to consensually postpone the discussion, so the interaction ended in not the best of terms.

In both cases, it is useful if we are able to switch to a different activity without a negative impact of the conflict even if the person we have unresolved conflict with is present, but more often when they are not. Obviously, if the issues are very important or if they were piling up for some time, it is more difficult to do so, but it is nevertheless important to be able to 'switch' to another activity and engage in it efficiently.

That does not mean that one should be avoid the issues nor neglect dealing with them at the appropriate moment. On the contrary, avoiding or neglecting important issues also undermines our ability to 'switch' to another activity while resolving or transforming conflicts improves our ability to do so.

Being able to 'switch' to another activity merely means that we are able to postpone dealing with the issues (if they are important, or dropping them if they are not) and focus on the task at hand for the time being in order to be efficient, but still be able to 'switch' back to dealing with that particular issue constructively at more appropriate moment.

The Ability to Ignore Negative Aspects of Interaction

Many times, communication includes a mixture of positive and negative aspects and one cannot respond to both at the same time. So, one inevitably chooses to which aspect one responds. The ability to ignore negative aspects of interaction and respond to positive ones, when communication includes both, is functional in such situations.

Usually, we are more inclined to respond to negative aspects since they are more salient. Or we suppress our response if we are not allowed to respond or if we fear consequences of such our response. None of these options is healthy nor functional.

Responding to the positive aspect and ignoring the negative one (for the time being at least), on the other hand, is both healthy and functional. That obviously does not prevent us from bringing the negative aspects up later on or from dealing with them constructively. However, it does contribute to a more positive atmosphere and fosters cooperation. It also helps prevent and recognize potential misunderstandings and misinterpretations of the other's behavior. Namely, when we respond to a positive aspect of interaction, it can become clear, as interaction unfolds, that the aspect which we perceived as negative was misunderstood (e.g. we perceived the other as hostile while they were actually afraid, or we perceived the other as impolite, but s/he was tired).

Obviously, if it seems important, we can also decide to bring up the negative aspect, but the key thing is that we do not have to focus on it if we decide it is not crucial. We can always, if we determine that it is important enough, bring it up later on or at another moment or even in the next situation when it occurs. But what is important is that it is our conscious decision to do so, and not because we are unable to 'let it go'.

The Ability to 'Switch' to Meta Level of Interaction

The ability to 'switch' to meta level of interaction means the ability to: switch to meta-communication that is communication about communication. Or if meta communication is for some reason not possible or appropriate, the ability to be aware of it observing and analyzing the communication, especially its aspects not related to content, for example the tone of communication, emotions, communication patterns, etc.

This ability is functional in two aspects. First, it creates a psychological distance from the situation, so we can observe what is happening more consciously and remain calmer. Secondly, it enables us to assess the situation more accurately and consequently respond to it more productively.

If also the other person is able to do the same, we can in most cases quickly fix or adjust our mode of communication to be more productive, or if needed postpone (or just drop) the discussion to a more appropriate moment, especially if there seems to be something that would take more time and energy to deal with, or if we got upset and need to calm down first.

Even if the other does not respond to our attempt of meta-communication, we can still benefit from that by remaining calmer and assessing the situation and consequently responding to it more functionally.

Elements of Conflict Sensitivity	Elements of Conflict Tolerance
• Awareness about the existence of conflicts The ability to: • sense and recognize conflicts when interaction is hindered • foresee conflicts which may occur • analyze development and elements of conflict • consider different meanings, points of view, convictions, positions and value systems • notice different understanding or interpretations	The ability to: • function despite conflict • disregard minor conflicts • drop less important issues • understand minor conflicts as information or means of communication • postpone dealing with an issue • 'switch' to another activity without the negative impact of conflict • ignore negative aspects of interaction • 'switch' to meta level of interaction

Table2: Elements of conflict sensitivity and conflict tolerance.

Influences on Conflict Tolerance

Conflict tolerance can be regarded as one's general capacity, that is how well he or she handles the 'heat of the conflict' in general but also as a current level of tolerance which varies in relation to different people, contexts, situations and one's own state.

Current level of conflict tolerance is influenced by several factors including:
- Previously (un)resolved conflicts in a particular relationship and in general
- Context (people or environment) and situation
- Psychological state (happy, optimistic, sad, angry, afraid, worried, etc.)
- Physiological state (tired, ill, hungry, sleepy, etc.)
- Transitions and change (coming home, arriving to work etc.)

It is important to be aware of the changing nature of conflict tolerance and one's own current state since when our tolerance is decreased, it is possible and wise to postpone dealing with a particular issue, which increases the chances that it will be resolved successfully.

Context

Context - in terms of people and environment that we are in - has a direct impact on our level of conflict tolerance, since conflict tolerance depends on specific types of interactions and people that we interact with. At work, for example we may have a different level of conflict tolerance than at home or with friends. However, also within the same environment (e.g. work) we may have different levels of conflict tolerance for interacting with different people or groups of people (e.g. boss, coworker, customers, team, etc.) and also with respect to a specific individual. For example, if something happened in interaction with one coworker, we may have handled it constructively, whereas if the same thing happened in interaction with another (and all the rest being the same), we might respond destructively.

Situation

Not only environment and people, also situations have impact on our level of conflict tolerance. Within the same environment and with the same people, there are many different situations that can occur. Furthermore, a change in situation can cause a change in the level of our conflict tolerance. For example, there is a difference if it is early morning or the end of the day; if we have a lot of tasks or there is not much to do; if there is time pressure or there is plenty of time, etc.

Psychological State

Psychological state is also a factor that affects our level of conflict tolerance. It is not as general as unresolved conflicts or context, for example, but it still affects the level of conflict tolerance in a specific moment or situation. Positive feelings (e.g. happiness, excitement, optimism, affection, etc.) in general raise our level of conflict tolerance, and negative feelings (e.g. sadness, anger, worry, fear, etc.) contribute to a lower level of conflict tolerance.

Physiological State

In addition to psychological state, physiological state also has an impact on the level of conflict tolerance. If one is hungry, ill, injured, sleepy, cold, etc., one is less able to tolerate the tension of conflict. On the other hand, if one is rested, full, warm and healthy, one can endure higher levels of tension and still preserve a constructive response.

Transitions

Transitions are a further factor in conflict tolerance. Normally not for long, but every change of environment presents at least a slight level of friction (e.g. coming home from work or coming to work from lunch break, etc.), since one has to reorganize the mode of functioning from one that is appropriate for one environment to one that is appropriate for the other. In this respect 10 to 20 minutes of transition time when the individual is not fully engaged is functional.

Change

Similar to transition, only in to a greater extent, any sort of change in the environment, either lasting or temporary, can also have an impact on our level of conflict tolerance, since change presents additional challenges or tasks that we have to deal with and accommodate, so there is less reserve for dealing with potential conflicts.

Previously (Un)Resolved Conflicts

Previous conflicts are also an important factor for the level of conflict tolerance, either resolved or unresolved. Previously unresolved conflicts, especially within the same relationship, tend to pile up (and 'ferment') and decrease our ability to deal with new (or old) issues constructively, therefore they diminish our conflict tolerance. One aspect of that influence is also the fact that (unresolved) conflicts are interconnected, so even if we start with one, other (directly or indirectly) related issues pop up, so the more unresolved conflicts we have, the more difficult it becomes to deal with them constructively. Namely, if we were not able to resolve a conflict at the time, it is even less likely to be able to do so together with an additional conflict.

On the other hand, every resolved or transformed conflict contributes to the increase in conflict tolerance in the very relationship or context that it was resolved and to our general level of conflict tolerance at the same time.

Aspect of Impact	Examples
Context	environment, group, social role, relationship
Situation	end of the day, huge amount of work, time pressure, break, etc.
Previously (un)resolved conflicts	in a particular relationship, in a particular environment, in general
Mood and emotional state	angry, sad, afraid, under stress, etc. happy, calm, optimistic, etc.
Physiological state	tired, ill, hungry, sleepy, etc. rested, healthy, full, etc.
Transitions and change	coming home, arriving to work, etc.

Table 3: Aspects and examples of impact on conflict tolerance

Assessing Conflict Competence

Conflict competence of individuals, as well as that of groups or organizations can be assessed in various ways. One of them is using the questionnaire presented below comprising 48 questions which measure conflict sensitivity and conflict tolerance, out of which the score result for conflict competence is calculated. If the questionnaire is administered to a group, conflict competence of a group can be calculated and analyzed as well.

If conflict competence is less than optimal, either one or both of the factors can be responsible. On the other hand, even if conflict competence is relatively high, one of the factors can still be suboptimal and consequently assessing that and working on improving it can have a huge impact on improving conflict competence in general.

Conflict Competence Questionnaire

A TSC-2017 questionnaire which can be used for assessing conflict competence is presented below. The questionnaire was developed on the basis of the concepts of conflict tolerance and conflict sensitivity as presented above and was successfully used for some research and also for self-assessment in coaching and training courses. The questionnaire is copyright material, therefore, please read the *Notes on copyright and permission to use* below, before using it other than for yourself.

It is important to note that the questionnaire can be used with respect to dealing with conflicts in a specific relationship or with respect to dealing with conflicts in a specific context (e.g. in the family, at the workplace, with friends, etc.) or in general. Consequently, the results can vary from relationship to relationship or from context to context for the same person.

Therefore, when assessing conflict competence, it is important to have in mind a specific relationship or a context that is the most relevant or for which we want to get the results.

After deciding on a specific context or relationship which you want to assess your conflict competence for, read each of the 48 statements and mark the degree to which you agree with the statement, i.e. how true is this statement for you, using the scale from -3 to +3, meaning: -3 strongly disagree, -2 disagree, -1 slightly disagree, 0 – do not know or cannot decide, 1 slightly agree, 2 agree, 3 strongly agree. After marking your agreement for all the statements, you can calculate the results using the instructions below.

Questionnaire: TSC-2017

1. Quarrels do not represent problems for me.	-3 -2 -1 0 1 2 3
2. Even when in conflict I have the wellbeing of the other in mind.	-3 -2 -1 0 1 2 3
3. After a fight I can easily switch to a different mood.	-3 -2 -1 0 1 2 3
4. When conflict occurs I gain energy.	-3 -2 -1 0 1 2 3
5. Conflicts are useful.	-3 -2 -1 0 1 2 3
6. Despite conflict I am able to function well.	-3 -2 -1 0 1 2 3
7. I am able to ignore minor conflicts.	-3 -2 -1 0 1 2 3
8. I am able to just let go of minor issues.	-3 -2 -1 0 1 2 3
9. I am able to perceive minor conflicts as messages and take them into account.	-3 -2 -1 0 1 2 3
10. I am able to postpone the dealing with conflict to later.	-3 -2 -1 0 1 2 3
11. I am able to switch to a different activity, without the prior conflict presenting a major difficulty.	-3 -2 -1 0 1 2 3
12. Already during conflict, I am able to look at it from the perspective of someone who is not involved.	-3 -2 -1 0 1 2 3

13. It would be better if there were no conflicts.	-3 -2 -1 0 1 2 3
14. I am afraid of conflicts.	-3 -2 -1 0 1 2 3
15. Conflicts are damaging.	-3 -2 -1 0 1 2 3
16. A fight makes me depressed and I stay depressed for a long time.	-3 -2 -1 0 1 2 3
17. After a fight I am angry at the other person for a long time.	-3 -2 -1 0 1 2 3
18. In a fight I sometimes lose control.	-3 -2 -1 0 1 2 3
19. In a fight I try to hurt or subordinate the other.	-3 -2 -1 0 1 2 3
20. If conflict occurs, I am not able to function normally.	-3 -2 -1 0 1 2 3
21. Very seldom am I able to look at the conflict from outside.	-3 -2 -1 0 1 2 3
22. If there is conflict, I lose energy.	-3 -2 -1 0 1 2 3
23. I get upset when there is conflict.	-3 -2 -1 0 1 2 3
24. Conflicts are detrimental for good relationships.	-3 -2 -1 0 1 2 3

25. I quickly notice if there is tension in communication.	-3 -2 -1 0 1 2 3
26. I notice possible misunderstandings.	-3 -2 -1 0 1 2 3
27. I notice sooner than others that two misunderstood each other.	-3 -2 -1 0 1 2 3
28. I can often foresee possible misunderstandings.	-3 -2 -1 0 1 2 3
29. I notice quickly if someone misunderstood what I said.	-3 -2 -1 0 1 2 3
30. I quickly assess if I can work well with someone or not.	-3 -2 -1 0 1 2 3
31. I soon realize which topics and which areas are difficult for the other person.	-3 -2 -1 0 1 2 3
32. In addition to the content, I also pay attention to how we talk to each other.	-3 -2 -1 0 1 2 3
33. I always allow for the possibility that the other has different view than me.	-3 -2 -1 0 1 2 3
34. I can change the topic even before tension occurs.	-3 -2 -1 0 1 2 3
35. Conflicts are present in every relationship and every group.	-3 -2 -1 0 1 2 3
36. I can often anticipate conflicts before they occur.	-3 -2 -1 0 1 2 3

37. Often I am not aware of the fact that the other does not share my thoughts.	-3 -2 -1 0 1 2 3
38. When conflict occurs, I usually do not know why it happened.	-3 -2 -1 0 1 2 3
39. I am afraid of conflicts.	-3 -2 -1 0 1 2 3
40. Conflicts are damaging and unnecessary.	-3 -2 -1 0 1 2 3
41. Only difficult people get involved in conflicts.	-3 -2 -1 0 1 2 3
42. In good relationships, there are no conflicts.	-3 -2 -1 0 1 2 3
43. Conflicts are in most cases related to physical or psychological abuse.	-3 -2 -1 0 1 2 3
44. I do not know, how to deal effectively with conflicts.	-3 -2 -1 0 1 2 3
45. Conflicts bring tension and pain.	-3 -2 -1 0 1 2 3
46. I do not know much about conflicts.	-3 -2 -1 0 1 2 3
47. Conflict means that it is not possible to talk any more.	-3 -2 -1 0 1 2 3
48. When talking, what matters most is the content and not so much the way we talk.	-3 -2 -1 0 1 2 3

Questionnaire: TSC-2017 © **Marko Iršič, 2017**

Calculating the Results

For calculating the results of this questionnaire, fill in below the results for each statement. Then sum up the results for each column, thus getting four numbers (A, B, C and D). Then calculate the result for Conflict Tolerance (CT=A-B), Conflict sensitivity (CS=C-D) and Conflict Competence (CC = CT + CS) as shown below.

Column A	Column B	Column C	Column D
Result for statement no.	Result for statement no.	Result for statement no.	Result for statement no.
1 : _____	13 : _____	25 : _____	37 : _____
2 : _____	14 : _____	26 : _____	38 : _____
3 : _____	15 : _____	27 : _____	39 : _____
4 : _____	16 : _____	28 : _____	40 : _____
5 : _____	17 : _____	29 : _____	41 : _____
6 : _____	18 : _____	30 : _____	42 : _____
7 : _____	19 : _____	31 : _____	43 : _____
8 : _____	20 : _____	32 : _____	44 : _____
9 : _____	21 : _____	33 : _____	45 : _____
10 : _____	22 : _____	34 : _____	46 : _____
11 : _____	23 : _____	35 : _____	47 : _____
12 : _____	24 : _____	36 : _____	48 : _____
Sum of col. A A= _____	Sum of col. B B= _____	Sum of col. C C= _____	Sum of col. D D= _____

Result for **Conflict Tolerance:** A – B = _____ (CT)

Result for **Conflict Sensitivity:** C – D = _____ (CS)

Result for **Conflict Competence:** CT + CS = _____ (CC)

Notes on Copyright and Permission to Use

The questionnaire presented above is copyright material and should not be used without permission by the author. Upon request, however, I will gladly give permission to use the questionnaire for the purpose of scientific research, provided that the results of the research will be submitted to me.

Similarly, I will give permission to use the questionnaire within the company that purchased this book for the purpose of assessing the level of conflict competence in the company, either to determine if some programs designed to raise conflict competence are in order, or for determining an impact of such programs (e.g. training courses, coaching, mediation etc.), provided that they will commit to send to me the results of the assessment (for research purposes) with general details of the company (e.g. no. of employees, years of existence, field of work etc.).

For other purposes (e.g. if a company or an individual wants to use the questionnaire as part of training courses, coaching or counseling that they provide or as a part of the hiring process or for assessing the level of conflict competence of individual clients or employees), a training in how to use the questionnaire and a license agreement is required.

For individuals, however, who bought this book for themselves or that got it as a present, I hereby give the permission to use the questionnaire for themselves personally (including their partners, family members and friends) without any obligation other than to protect the copyright.

How to Use the Questionnaire?

The questionnaire can be used in various ways, depending on the context and the intention. Is it for the purposes of the assessment in the company or is it for personal use? Is it used anonymously or as part of a development or a training process, etc.

As already pointed out, a training course on how to use this questionnaire and a license agreement are generally required. With respect to the examples above, where the permission for use is or shall be given upon request, I briefly present some guidelines below.

If it is used for assessment purposes within an organization or department, it should be done anonymously, without collecting personal information of employees, which would make it possible to identify individuals (e.g. name, date of birth, address, etc.). However, including items like gender, age, department, position, etc., is permitted. The goal of the assessment (e.g. assessing the general level of conflict competence in the organization or assessing the general improvement of conflict competence after the implementation of a specific program) should be clearly communicated to respondents and the questionnaire should be distributed to them simultaneously and collected without marking who submitted specific questionnaires. If employees think that they are being evaluated individually, they might be more inclined to submit more favorable answers, and consequently the reliability of such assessment would be compromised.

The use for research purposes is largely determined by researchers' practice and depends also on specific research design, so it will not be commented upon here. However, consultations on how to use the questionnaire within a specific research field are possible.

For personal use on the other hand, one can use it for self-assessment and also for determining potential areas of personal development.

One can have in mind a specific relationship (e.g. spouse, child, friend, etc.) or context (home, work, friends, etc.) or life in general and can fill in the questionnaire with that in mind. One can also fill in the questionnaire with different relationships or contexts in mind to obtain results relevant for that context or relationship. After calculating the result (as described above), one can also review the responses and determine which are the areas that contribute the most to a lower level of conflict competence, e.g. conflict sensitivity or conflict tolerance, but also individual parameters or items in the questionnaire.

An additional option to use, within a trusting relationship (e.g. spouses, siblings, parent and child, friends, etc.), is to ask the other that they fill in the questionnaire for us like they perceive us with the same context in mind. Then the results can be compared and additional insights gained. Partners can, for example, also do that for each other, so they both gain additional insights and assessment of their potential areas of growth.

Ranks of Conflict Competence

In terms of levels of score results for conflict competence we can categorize results into seven ranks: less than 0 points (extremely low conflict competence), from 0 to 19 points (very low conflict competence), from 20 to 39 points (low conflict competence), from 40 to 59 points (medium conflict competence), from 60 to 79 points (high conflict competence), from 80 to 99 points (very high conflict competence) and 100 points or more (extremely high conflict competence), presented in Table 4.

Result	Rank of Conflict Competence
Less than 0	extremely low
0 to 19	very low
20 to 39	low
40 to 59	medium
60 to 79	high
80 to 99	very high
100 or more	extremely high

Table 4: Categories of score-results for Conflict Competence

Types of People with Respect to Conflict Tolerance and Conflict Sensitivity

In relation to conflict tolerance and conflict sensitivity there are four types of people: l*eaders, loners, exploited and conflictually challenged* (Iršič, 2004). Obviously, that can be a general trait, but can also vary from context to context or from one relationship to another.

Leaders have both, high conflict tolerance and high conflict sensitivity. They are not necessarily formal leaders, but they nevertheless have important impact on others related to their area, either professional or personal. They can either lead by example or they can have an impact by directing or helping others figure out how to deal with issues they face.

Loners have high conflict sensitivity, but low conflict tolerance. Therefore, they are quick to withdraw or avoid conflict interaction. They can prosper in activities which do not rely on direct interaction with others.

Exploited have high tolerance and low sensitivity. Consequently, they can endure much, but do not perceive something as conflict or something that could be dealt with. They just accept it.

Conflictually challenged have low tolerance, meaning they are quick to become destructive, but also low sensitivity, thus they do not perceive something as conflict but rather (not unlike the exploited) as part of reality which is difficult or threatening. Consequently, they develop dysfunctional response to conflicts, either at the expense of their health (either physical or psychological), at the expense of their relationships (having a few, if any, good relationships) or at the expense of others (abusing or intimidating others).

Improving Conflict Competence

Conflict competence is an important trait of individuals (and consequently groups, organizations or societies) and it can have a strong impact on the quality of interactions and relationships, and consequently on the quality of life in general. Therefore, it is important to know how one can improve or develop conflict competence.

Below there are some guidelines and descriptions on how to develop conflict competence, presented separately for conflict sensitivity and for conflict tolerance. Obviously, raising any of those has an impact on conflict competence, but it is nevertheless important to have both sufficiently developed. By self-assessment using the questionnaire above, one can determine which fields are more important to focus on, in order to develop it the most.

The activities for raising conflict competence are by no means unconnected to each other. Some activities develop both, tolerance and sensitivity at the same time, or the development of a skill within conflict sensitivity, for example, raises conflict tolerance as a side effect as well. Others, on the other hand, may have a major impact only on one of them.

Focusing primarily on the aspect (tolerance or sensitivity) which we determined is less developed (e.g. by achieving a lower score in the questionnaire), has a stronger impact on our overall ability to deal successfully with conflicts.

Some of the proposals below are accompanied with examples or possible exercises, while for the others a mere description is given. Irrespective of that, it is important to develop general traits (e.g. sensitivity and tolerance) and not focus strongly only on one or a few exercises.

The guidelines and proposals below are not meant as a comprehensive manual, but rather as explanations and illustrations of specific activities that can contribute to the improvement of conflict sensitivity or conflict tolerance. One can design a variety of exercises with the same objective and also combine or modify them. The overall goal, however, is raising conflict competence, rather than developing any given skill per se.

Improving Conflict Sensitivity

Conflict sensitivity can be systematically improved, inter alia, by (self)observation and analysis of our own conflicts (successfully resolved and also unresolved) or those we witness either in our surroundings or in movies, literature, talk shows, news etc., learning (through books, articles, videos, seminars, workshops and training courses), practical, written (e.g. transcribing conflict interaction) or mental exercises.

All the above expand and differentiate our understanding and awareness of conflicts and related concepts and phenomena, and consequently improve our conflict sensitivity.

Accepting Conflicts as Part of Reality

The first step for raising conflict sensitivity is obviously accepting the fact that conflicts are a normal part of reality, not a deviation but a common ingredient. Perceiving them as normal and not as a deviation or a catastrophe changes our awareness and perception. Since we are not afraid, we can see things more objectively and become more aware of the existence and presence of conflicts. Consequently, we can more easily notice them when they appear and understand that they are present.

(Self)Observation

A further step is observation. Just observing the facts. What is happening? What are the differences? How is interaction developing? What are things that seem to be repeating themselves in terms of contents and in terms of patterns? Which are the 'hot' or sensitive topics? Just observing, without judgment or trying to change.

And observing ourselves: How am I behaving or responding to the situation? How do I talk? What do I say? How do I feel? What am I afraid of? What hurt me? What do I want to avoid? What do I want to accomplish?

By practicing observation and self-observation we improve our conflict sensitivity, so we can notice conflicts and their elements more easily and sooner. By the same token, our conflict tolerance improves as well, since already by adopting the observation stance, we distance ourselves emotionally from the situation and at the same time we decrease the automatic reaction, thus we can have more control over our responses, which is obviously functional if our emotions and automatic responses are destructive. It does not mean suppressing emotions, just observing ourselves and the situation, which by itself decreases the intensity of emotions and automatic responses.

As an exercise one can mentally observe a conflict, either one that is happening or one that has happened in the past, by observing it as if one departed from their own body and observed the situation from outside. It takes some practice to be able to do that in conflict, but it is fairly easy to do it in one's mind. Obviously, the image of the conflict is going to be blurry or confused, but that is not the point and with practice the picture will become clearer and more accurate. The point is to be able to adopt the observing stance consciously with respect to conflict at hand and thereby gradually raising conflict sensitivity.

Analysis of Our Own Conflicts

Another aspect of developing conflict sensitivity is the analysis of conflicts in terms of interaction and in terms of content (incompatibilities).

How did the conflict start? When did it start? What triggered it? How did the interaction unfold? How did it end? How much of conscious or automatic interaction was there? Where were the opportunities to change the course of interaction?

Which topics or issues were involved? Was the discussion structured or was it chaotic? Were the emotions intense or moderate? Did it end successfully or consensually or was the interaction interrupted?

Again, with this analysis, it is important to be as objective as possible. Merely describing or determining the issues and patterns as facts, similar to someone neutral describing them. A good indication of that is the question: Would the other one describe it the same way or could s/he agree with my description? If possible, it is very useful to compare or discuss descriptions with the other and accept as facts only those parts that both agree are factual.

It is important to analyze unresolved conflicts or interaction that went wrong, but also successfully resolved conflicts. By analyzing both and comparing them, we can discover some additional opportunities to act differently next time.

Most of the time, when conflict escalates, it also quickly expands, meaning that suddenly many issues are involved at the same time. Since that is so overwhelming, the interaction is many times ended or suppressed without any progress in order to prevent it from escalating even further, and this only contributes to a similar conflict situation occurring over and over again. A mere list of issues made after an argument, could help in terms of dealing with the conflict better and in terms of raising conflict sensitivity.

Analysis of Conflicts We Witness

In addition to analyzing our own conflicts, it is useful to analyze also conflicts that we are not involved in. In fact, it is much easier to do so and to remain objective than to analyze our own conflicts. However, those conflicts that are similar to ours, have a tendency of drawing us to one side of the argument, so if that happens, this is a sure sign that we have to deal with that issue ourselves. We can observe conflicts in our surroundings, family, at workplace, among our friends, etc. However, in any case it is important to remain neutral and distance ourselves from the content, and rather observe the patterns of interaction, the issues that were addressed, the development of conversation, etc.

Analysis of Conflicts in Art, Media and Literature

Furthermore, art, media and literature are also a good source of material for the analysis of conflicts, for example, movies, novels, theatre shows, talk shows, round tables, discussions, the news and also scientific, professional and self-help literature. With these cases, we can practice analyzing objectively in order to develop our ability. With these cases, there is an additional advantage, namely, we can revisit them several times (e.g. read again, replay, listen again, etc.), which is normally not possible with live conflicts.

Learning about Conflicts

In addition to the analysis of conflict we engage in, witness or perceive through art, media and literature, a further possibility to raise our conflict sensitivity is by learning about conflicts, not only in terms of specific skills of dealing with them, but also in terms of understanding them better. To learn the dynamics and patterns of conflicts and communication for that matter. By understanding them better, we can see more clearly what is going on and by knowing the dynamics, we can foresee certain conflicts or misunderstandings.

Practical and Mental Exercises

In addition to real conflicts we engage in or witness, practical exercises or role plays with reflection and analyses are a good source of raising conflict sensitivity. Since the situations are not real but simulated, they are easier to analyze objectively, and at the same time we gain insight in our own patterns of responding to conflict.

In addition to practical, also mental exercises are useful. When imagining certain situations, for example, we can control our imagination. We can slow down the process, 'rewind', stop, rerun, etc., and we can also take time to analyze it.

Writing Exercises

In addition to mental exercises, also written exercises (e.g. transcribing conflict interaction) are useful in this respect. The method of giving each party in the conflict a task to write down what happened, could be used in this context. However, such a task is often given to gain information and to be able to decide who is at fault. Obviously, that does not serve the same purpose.

Writing down, not with the intention of determining who is at fault, but with the intention of understanding and being aware of what is or was going on, has a potential of raising conflict sensitivity.

Another example of a written exercise would be writing down the issues or topics that were discussed, and listing the disagreements (as well as possible agreements) which were involved in the interaction. Rarely, there is a conflict over only one thing, rather when conflict starts, there is abundance of issues involved. That is also why it is usually so overwhelming on the one hand, but also why it presents a good opportunity for developing conflict sensitivity in terms of seeing various issues or topics and being able to distinguish between them and deal with them consciously.

Many times, people do not even remember what happened or they have a distorted recollection of facts. Moreover, they do not hear what was said, but they tend to add - without realizing it - their interpretation and attribute a meaning to it which it may not have.

That is why it is useful to practice writing down or transcribing a discussion, since by that we sharpen our skill of perceiving precisely what is going on and being able to see it more clearly. Practicing writing down, therefore, is more important than getting it right each time. Namely, by practice our accuracy improves as well, and the goal is to develop the ability to accurately perceive or recollect what is or was happening.

Strengthening the Ability to Sense, Recognize and Foresee Conflicts

When interaction is hindered, there is a good chance that there is a conflict or incompatibility underneath. Developing a habit of looking below the disruption in order to recognize conflicts, can contribute to our capacity to sense and recognize conflicts and also foresee conflicts which may occur. When we notice disruption in communication, we can ask ourselves: What is the incompatibility below this disruption? Are there any differences involved? Is the interaction productive or unproductive? Do we all interact from the state of strength and responsiveness or is there weakness and self-absorption present? Already by consciously focusing our attention on these aspects, we improve our recognition capacity, and we also improve our ability to foresee such situations in the future. At the same time, focusing the attention consciously on the source of disruption or incompatibility can instantly increase our conflict tolerance as well, since it diminishes the impact of the tension arising from such incompatibility by consciously observing it and by that psychologically distancing oneself from it.

Consciously Considering Different Meanings, Points of View, Convictions, Positions and Value Systems

Developing the ability to consider different aspects obviously takes some practice until it becomes a habit to have an open mind. Believing in only one correct interpretation or truth is somewhat at odds with an open mind, however it is not contrary. One can believe in one thing but still have an open mind.

A very useful technique is 'what if …' in terms what if that were true (e.g. What if the world was indeed flat?). It obviously goes both ways (e.g. The one who believes that the world is flat, can consider what if it was round?)

By consciously considering different meanings, points of view, etc., we also strengthen our ability to notice different understandings or interpretations as they occur. Obviously, by not allowing for differences and assuming that we all hold the same positions, understandings, etc., we are less likely to notice the differences also when they actually occur.

> **Improving Conflict Sensitivity**
> - Accepting conflicts as part of reality
> - (Self)observation
> - Analysis of our own conflicts
> - Analysis of conflicts we witness
> - Analysis of conflicts in art, media and literature
> - Learning about conflicts
> - Practical and mental exercises
> - Writing exercises
> - Strengthening the ability to sense, recognize and foresee conflicts
> - Consciously considering different meanings, points of view, convictions, positions and value systems

Table 5: Elements of improving conflict sensitivity

Raising Conflict Tolerance

We can raise our conflict tolerance by getting used to (smaller) conflicts (in terms not being afraid of them) and acquiring and practicing skills for dealing with conflicts (at training courses, workshops, with colleagues, on our own by mental practice or in real situations where we apply appropriate skills).

In addition to acquiring and practicing skills, each successfully resolved conflict (even if small) contributes to increased conflict tolerance especially in the same relationship or context.

Furthermore, practicing conscious choices in conflict, focusing on the current activity and consciously deciding on the importance of conflicts and issues can help.

Additional means to improve conflict tolerance are changing the perspective (e.g. looking at the same situation from the future) or a broader context (seeing the conflict situation together with other aspects and situations in a specific relationship or environment).

Furthermore, individual or joint reflection and analysis of the interaction and outcome of both successfully resolved and unresolved conflicts is very functional in this respect.

In addition, also switching out of conflict and consciously focusing on positive aspects of interaction are very important practices.

The key aspect of improving conflict tolerance, however, is accepting the responsibility for our actions and responses (including thoughts and emotions) and leaving the responsibility for their responses and behavior, thinking and emotions to the others.

Getting Used to Conflicts

In general people are afraid of conflicts and perceive them as something bad. Consequently, they tend to avoid conflict interaction and feel helpless when it occurs. In addition, people try to end it as soon as possible. Consequently, they do not learn how to understand conflict dynamics, nor do they use the situation for practicing skills.

Getting used to conflicts in a sense that we do not perceive and experience them as something terrible is functional with respect to developing conflict tolerance. Practicing experiencing conflicts and still remaining calm as much as possible contributes also to being able to consciously observe what is going on.

By consciously observing the situation and interaction which we are involved in – rather than automatically reacting - we also, as already mentioned, distance ourselves emotionally from it and consequently increase the possibility of consciously choosing our response as well.

Practicing conscious choice is in itself productive, since even if we make a wrong decision, while believing it would be functional, we can make a different choice next time.

Accepting Responsibility

A fundamental strategy for raising conflict tolerance is accepting responsibility. Not necessarily for the situation as such, but certainly for our response to it in terms of actions, words, emotions and thoughts. A situation may happen, but it is up to us how we respond. The reason it seems that the other caused our response is that the response pattern is many times automatic and subconscious. However, consciously accepting the responsibility for our responses, albeit hard to do, is strongly liberating and empowering. It is we who decide how we will respond and the first step is owning to our response and deciding if it is such that we want to repeat in future situations or we want to change it.

Leaving the Responsibility for Their Actions and Feelings to Others

Seemingly contrary to the guideline above, but also crucial to raising conflict tolerance is letting others do the same - accept responsibility. And to do so, our role is to not take the responsibility from them. Certainly, we can impact others to a certain extent, but ultimately we cannot control their thoughts, emotions and actions, so what they do, say, think or feel is ultimately up to them.

By doing so we also avoid being victims of emotional blackmailing (Forward & Fraizer, 1998) in terms: If you do not do what I want you to, I will be hurt or upset! Obviously, I am not saying that one should act carelessly, behave badly or even intentionally do things that upset the others and then state as an excuse that it is the others who are responsible for their feelings and responses. But at the same time, we should not refrain from doing something that is good or important to us out of fear of hurting the others' feelings, for example.

If we want to help them take responsibility (which would be empowering for them), we certainly should remain calm ourselves. We can also check with them about what they want or how they want to act, feel and think. And by that, we help them see they have a choice. For example, we can ask them: *Do you want to be upset?* or *Do you want to shout?* or *Do you want to be hurt?*, etc.

Such help is not always possible or wanted, so we have to also accept if they reject our attempts and not try to impose it in order to impose change in their response. In any case, it is important, however, that we leave the choice to them, and that we are not emotionally dependent on how they decide.

Understanding Dynamics and Patterns of Conflict

When dealing with a difficult situation, it is useful if we understand the situation and what is going on in order to be able to act competently. Understanding the patterns and dynamics of conflict helps us orient ourselves in conflict situations and act constructively. It helps us choose the right responses for the situation. Namely, not understanding what is going on, can contribute to us acting in a manner that only makes the matters worse. And our automatic responses are usually doing precisely that, making the matters worse.

For starters, already reading chapter one of this book can help understand a little bit more the characteristics and the dynamics of conflict, but there are many more books, audio and video programs and training courses that can help us understand the dynamics of conflict better.

Practicing Conscious Choices in Conflict

Our interaction is mostly automatic, and even more so the conflict interaction. If it is constructive, it is all good and well, but it is different when it is destructive. Since it is automatic for the most part, the more so the more intense the conflict, we have little or no choice on how to act (even if it seems we do). That is also why later on we regret saying or doing what we did. In practice, even if they regret doing or saying something, people for the most part do not prepare and even less practice a different response for the next time in a such situation, therefore it is most likely that the automatic response is going to be the same as in the past.

Imagining the same situation and asking ourselves how we want to respond next time, and even how we want to feel next time in such a situation is the first step. If we do not know the answer to that, we will repeat the usual automatic responses and probably regret them later. When we decide on our response, we need to check with ourselves if we are going to be OK with such a response and if it is going to be good for people close to us. If the answer to either is no, we might want to find another response which would suit the situation better.

For example, if when criticized, we explode and verbally attack the other, we might want to change our response to just being quiet, but this repeatedly fails. After checking with ourselves, if we are OK with such a response, we might find out that this is not the case and we might decide to try to listen actively and even politely ask the one that is (allegedly) criticizing us for additional, specific explanation.

After we determine a response which we are happy with, we still need to practice it, so it becomes automatic at least to a certain degree. We can practice that in our mind, by imagining a situation and then imagining our new response and observe how it works. We could also practice such a new response in a simulated situation (e.g. at a workshop or a training course or with a friend), or we can practice it in a real situation, either when it happens next time or, if appropriate (e.g. with the spouse or a friend), practice in advance with the person where such response is planned. For example, after determining and agreeing on a new response, we can say: Let's try it out next time!

Obviously, practicing in advance with the same person is not always possible especially if the relationship is not close or good. In that case, however, we can still practice it in our mind and in a simulated situation, and by that we change our response unilaterally.

Metacommunication, Reflection and Analysis of the Interaction

By conscious practice of analyzing the interaction, we develop the ability to 'switch to' the meta level. It is useful at any point of time, but the sooner we do it, the better it is. And the analysis of interaction means precisely that: analyzing interaction, not analyzing the other or even plotting a revenge of a sort. It also does not include feeling sorry for oneself, but just trying to make a factual 'recollection' of events and estimating where it went wrong and list the opportunities where it could be different. Usually, when we are in a destructive conflict, we feel frustration and we rarely observe interaction objectively. Consequently, we act in ways which do not make sense, and so does the other side.

It is useful to analyze both successfully resolved and unresolved conflicts individually and if possible also together with the other person(s). We can, for example, write down or transcribe the conversation, and discover the opportunities where we (rather than the other) could have chosen a different, more constructive response to the situation and the other's behavior or words, and what that response might be.

Talking regularly about the quality of our communication, functional as well as dysfunctional patterns, listing or mapping (not talking trough) our differences, emotional responses and habits, etc., either with the person that they are relevant for or with someone else (e.g. a mediator, a coach, a therapist, a friend, etc.), or analyzing those by ourselves (e.g. writing a journal, sketching a map, describing a pattern, etc.), contributes to our ability to switch to the meta level of interaction in general, but also when we are in conflict or shortly afterwards.

Switching to the meta level of interaction and the analysis becomes easier also in conflict, when it is regularly practiced. Most of the time we interact with being focused on tasks, goals and content, therefore many times we are not conscious of the way we interact. Even when in conflict we are still focused on the content to the extent that we do not notice that the interaction is becoming progressively more destructive. It is only when we are deep in a destructive interaction that we switch the awareness to our frustration which "came from nowhere", and consequently, it is easier to blame it on the other, since we have no idea how we came there.

The irony is that the same type of communication which is functional when there is no conflict, can be counterproductive when conflict occurs. For example, explaining our position is functional when there is no conflict and the other(s) are willing to listen, as opposed to explaining our position when there is a conflict and the other(s) want to prove their point and are not willing to listen. In addition, when frustrated people tend to repeat and even intensify the same actions, or give up, neither of which helps in resolving the problem.

Practicing periodically to focus on the quality of interaction, the inner sense of strength and responsiveness, the patterns of communication, the differences and similarities in statements and other aspects of interaction with respect to conflict, and also on other constructive or cooperative examples of interaction and communication, contributes to the development of skill and the capacity to easily switch to the meta-level. The activities that can help us with that are also the analysis of conflicts that we are engaged in, that we witness or those in art and media, as described in the previous chapter.

Consciously Focusing on the Current Activity

The ability to function in spite of conflict and the ability to postpone dealing with a particular issue are both related to the ability to separate between what we are doing at the moment and the other aspects of our lives, which means being able to set aside or postpone dealing with other issues. When we are, for example, unable to resist thinking about something, it has much to do with rejecting the reality (it should not be like that), on the one hand, and with failing to consciously decide on how important this is, how to go about it and allocating the time to think about it, on the other. If we decide it is not important, we can just disregard or drop it, if it is important, however, we have to make a plan on how to go about it. Sometimes just deciding on the time (e.g. in the evening or during lunch break) when to think about it and making a plan can suffice, other times it might be necessary to make a list of things that are bothering us, or even creating a list of tasks related to it may be needed to be able to postpone it. In any case, consciously accepting it and allocating mental space to it is important. Just trying to suppress issues, if they are important, does not work. So already by practicing treating (important) conflicts as tasks to deal with and possibly listing them, we get a strong impact on our ability to focus on the task at hand and to postpone dealing with the conflict.

Consciously Deciding on the Importance of Conflicts and Issues

Asking oneself about the importance of a certain conflict or issue, and consciously deciding about it, has a direct impact on our further functioning. If we determine it is important, we will have to deal with it eventually, one way or another. If we decide they are not important, on the other hand, we can easily drop or disregard them or understand them as information or means of communication.

The distinction between dropping less important issues and disregarding smaller conflict lies in the focus on the content or the quality of interaction, respectively. If the content of our conflict is not important, we can drop the issue, but if the conflict is not minor (e.g. if the other is hurt), we cannot simply disregard it, but we need to restore constructive interaction (sometimes just taking something back or apologizing suffices, other times a more thorough process is needed). On the other hand, if the conflict is minor but the content is important, we can disregard the conflict or understand it as information (e.g. he did not like that), but still continue (then or later) dealing with the issues which are important

Acquiring and Practicing Skills

Acquiring and practicing skills for dealing with conflicts is obviously also an important part of raising conflict tolerance, since being able to deal skillfully with a situation also helps us to be able to tolerate a higher degree of conflict. There are many training courses where one can learn useful skills (for example, mediation training courses, training courses in communication wellness, training courses in communication skills, training courses in conflict resolution skills, etc.). In addition to training courses, there are also workshops and seminars offered on the same topics. Furthermore, one can learn the skills to a certain extent also using audio or video learning materials and even books or articles. In addition, we can also test and practice the newly acquired skills either at training courses or with colleagues, or also on our own by mental practice, and use the skills progressively more competently in real situations where conflict occurs. If we perceive the real-life conflicts as training opportunities, this does not only increase the efficiency of skills acquisition but also instantly raises our conflict tolerance in that situation.

Let's do that Again!

Depending on the circumstances, it is sometimes possible and appropriate to just repeat the last part of interaction in a more appropriate way. If we realize that the last part played out the way we did not want it, we can propose: *Let's do that again!* Obviously, it works better if both sides are aware and agree in advance on this, however, it is possible to also do it with people who are not (yet) used to it! After proposing that, we can just repeat the last part of the interaction in a new, more productive way which we would have wanted to use in the first place. That changes direction of the current interaction, but also reinforces a new pattern of interaction for the future.

Successfully Resolved Conflicts

Every successfully resolved conflict (even if minor) contributes to increased conflict tolerance at least in two ways. Firstly, it decreases the amount of weight that unresolved conflicts contribute to the lowering of conflict tolerance, especially in the same relationship or context. Secondly, it means that we successfully used our skills in order to resolve the conflict and consequently are at least a little bit more able to use them next time in a similar situation.

However, this is easier said than done. Namely, as already mentioned, conflicts are interconnected and even when we start with one, others soon emerge (conflict expansion) and contribute to a more chaotic interaction and its intensity (conflict escalation). This is also why dealing with conflicts is less appealing than it should be. To overcome this obstacle, rather than suffering unresolved conflicts and paying the price for it, one can use mediation or communication wellness or transformative coaching, since it is easier to gradually resolve issues with the help of a trained professional than on our own.

'Switching out of Conflict'

A common phenomenon is that even if we are engaged in a less than optimal interaction, when someone else calls - whom we are not in conflict with - we are able to immediately switch to a different mode of interaction. This means that we do have the ability to do so, only we are not necessarily aware of it and we do not consciously practice it.

Switching out of conflict is also possible or easier if we understand conflict as a mode of interaction rather than the other person's fault. If it is a mode of interaction, we can change it (as in consciously changing our tone of voice) but if it is the other person's fault, we cannot do anything about it.

Consciously switching out of conflict either when changing the activity or even when we are continuing the interaction with the same person/s (which is obviously more difficult), strengthens also our ability to switch to the meta level of interaction and to 'switch' to another activity without a negative impact of the conflict.

Consciously Focusing on Constructive Aspects

The ability to ignore negative aspects of interaction and respond to positive ones when communication includes both can be practiced by consciously focusing on the positive ones. In every interaction there are positive aspects of interaction even if at first glance it does not seem so. The reason lies in the negative aspects being more salient. By being consciously focused and even searching for positive aspects, we increase the amount of those we notice on the one hand, and we also contribute to the increase of their amount, on the other.

For example, if someone is criticizing us, we can either respond at the perceived attack (and counterattack, defend ourselves or reject the other) or thank the other for feedback or information. If the other's intentions were good, they will be 'rewarded' by our response, and if they were not, they will not be successful. At the same time, we will not be upset in either case, and will contribute to preventing unproductive interaction or to fostering constructive communication with that person.

Sometimes people who are able to do that without necessarily knowing how, try to 'instruct' others that they should be more patient or tolerant, which only adds to their frustration, since they understand it as having to take and suppress even more destructiveness. What both fail to understand is that it is not about enduring or suppressing the pain, but about neutrallizing or not being negatively affected by it, which is a skill that can also be learned, it is only that neither side knows how.

Raising Conflict Tolerance
- Getting used to conflicts
- Accepting responsibility
- Leaving the responsibility for their actions and feelings to the others
- Understanding the dynamics and patterns of conflict
- Practicing conscious choices in conflict
- Metacommunication, reflection and analysis of the interaction
- Consciously focusing on the current activity
- Consciously deciding on the importance of conflicts and issues
- Acquiring and practicing skills
- Let's do that again!
- Successfully resolved conflicts
- 'Switching out of conflict'
- Consciously focusing on constructive aspects

Table 6: Elements of raising conflict tolerance

Managing Conflict Tolerance

In addition of improving conflict tolerance in general and in a specific context or relationship, managing it is also a very important set of skills. Conflict tolerance as mentioned above is susceptible to influence from various factors (physiological, psychological, situational, etc), therefore taking those into account can drastically improve efficiency of dealing with conflicts.

Taking Influences into Account

It makes a huge difference if we deal with conflicts when we feel OK or when our physiological state is not so good (e.g. hungry, ill, cold, tired, etc.), so checking with oneself – and with the other for that matter – how one feels can give us valuable information. Asking oneself and the other if one feels up to the task of dealing with a specific issue is another useful thing.

Similarly, taking into account the psychological state of all involved is important. It is the best if we choose a time when we are calm and so is the other. If we are under stress, upset, anxious, worried, etc., our conflict tolerance is diminished, so it is not the best time. On the other hand, if we are happy, excited, enthusiastic, etc., it is also not the best time to deal with a difficult issue, since dealing with a difficult issue will most likely undermine those positive feelings.

Checking with oneself and with the other about how they feel is useful in at least two ways. Firstly, it gives the opportunity to become aware of our psychological and physiological state, which is empowering in itself, so we are more able to deal with conflict. Secondly, we can consciously decide whether we are up to dealing with conflict at that time, or it would be better to postpone it. At the same time, already by asking that question, sometimes the conflict can actually dissolve.

Similarly, asking oneself and the other whether they are up to dealing with a specific issue, gives them a choice to deal with it or postpone the issue, which increases the sense of control over situation and instantly raises our conflict tolerance. Even if we choose to postpone the issue, however, we are already confronted with it and can already think about it, so it is even possible that it gets resolved indirectly, without necessarily discussing it or with a minimal time of discussion. Even if a longer discussion is needed, it is still dealt with at least to a certain extent by the time we decide to talk about it.

One could even take it for a rule, never to start dealing with a difficult issue before asking oneself and the other about how they feel and if they are up to it.

As regards transitions (e.g. when coming home or leaving home for that matter, coming to work, etc.), they are not the best time to deal with difficult issues. So, we can manage our conflict tolerance merely by avoiding dealing with conflict or other delicate issues, for example, within 20 minutes after arriving or when preparing to leave.

In terms of context (the environment or the relationship) or situation, we can manage our conflict tolerance by taking them into account in combination with other factors (e.g. psychological or physiological aspects) and, consequently, decide whether it is a good idea to deal with a certain issue on the spot, later on or perhaps we even propose mediation in order to make sure that things do not turn out worse.

Changing the Perspective

Changing the perspective is also a strong tool for raising conflict tolerance in general and also in a specific situation. One can observe the same situation from the outside, or tries to imagine how it would seem to someone else. Or one can imagine that s/he is looking at the same situation from the future and assessing its importance. Few things are actually so important that we would consider them worthwhile after several years, they only seem so at the moment, since we feel them intensely. Therefore, changing the perspective can help us perceive the situation more realistically and less emotionally.

Practicing a skill of changing perspective in a specific situation or a habit to shift perspectives especially when conflict occurs, contributes to raising our general level of conflict tolerance. Changing perspective is a skill which is not connected to a specific content or situation but is rather universally applicable and especially useful in conflicts.

Destructive conflict interaction has a tendency to prevent perspective shifts and to constrain us to only one valid perception of the situation which is functional in terms of quick or automatic response, but at the same time prevents us from correcting our erroneous assessment or incorrect perception of the situation, which only contributes to conflict escalation. The practice or habit of using various perspectives, especially in conflict situations is therefore a direct antidote to destructive conflict interaction.

Broader Context

Conflict tolerance can be greatly improved just by looking at the situation in a broader context. A conflict interaction often absorbs our attention and we feel like the conflict is overwhelming. Consequently, we feel frustrated and powerless.

In reality however, any individual conflict interaction, especially if it happens periodically, in most cases does not have a major negative impact on either the relationship or individuals involved. In most cases, especially in lasting relationships, life goes back on track after some time (e.g. after a few minutes, a few hours or in worst cases a few days).

Therefore, a habit of seeing a conflict situation together with the other aspects and situations in a specific relationship or environment can by itself dramatically improve our conflict tolerance. When we are in a conflict, we can, for example, think of the time after the conflict that will be calm again, which will instantly reorient our behavior and our attitude to the other and help us overcome the conflict sooner. Or we can think about our general satisfaction with that relationship and compare it to the current situation. Or we can think of good qualities that the other person has, etc. All such responses increase our conflict tolerance and make it easier to respond constructively to the situation, since our attention is no longer absorbed only in the current moment.

Preserving or Regaining Internal Stability

Preserving or regaining internal stability has a huge impact on our conflict tolerance. As described before, when people interact from a state of strength and responsiveness, interaction tends to be constructive, and when people interact from a state of weakness (and self absorption) interaction tends to be destructive. So merely making sure we are interacting from a state of strength (preserving internal stability) is a huge factor of preserving or regaining constructive interaction. The key aspect of preserving or regaining internal stability, however, is the distinction between our response and the others' behavior, words or emotions, as already discussed earlier (under the heading *Accepting Responsibility*).

It is not true that the behavior of others causes our responses, but it is a matter of an automatic response to behavior, words and even emotions of others. For example, if someone calls us "an idiot", we feel hurt or angry. If it is automatic, however, it does not mean that we have no control over it. It only means that our automatic response is triggered when a certain thing happens. Even if we do not know it, we can still decide how we will respond.

In order to change our automatic response, we need to, either consciously decide on our response in each situation (which is hard), or we can change our automatic response to the stimuli (which requires conscious analysis, choice and practicing the new response), or we can just create a distance between stimuli and our response. There are many methods and techniques of doing that, so we can choose amongst them. One relatively simple one is asking oneself: Why should I feel bad (e.g. sad, upset, angry, hurt, etc.) if she/he/they ... (... meaning whatever they do or say). For example: Why should I be hurt if he called me an idiot?

In addition, many times, especially when in conflict, we perceive things as more important than they actually are. For example, if others do or say something and we feel upset or hurt, often the reason is, that we treat the situation as very important and therefore it has more of effect on us. However, we can change our response. One way of changing it is asking ourselves: Is this what was dome or said very bad? In most cases the answer is "No", so we could just relax. But even if the answer is "Yes" we can at least realistically prepare and devise a plan for dealing with the consequences.

On the other hand, sometimes our emotional response is just dysfunctional. In such a case, we can ask ourselves for example: If I feel like this: Are things going to be any better because of that?

Are we going to get along better? Are things going to be resolved faster or more easily? Am I going to feel better because of that? Is there any reason whatsoever that I should feel like this? If the answer to all of these questions is no, there is a good chance that it does not make sense to feel that way. And at the same time, asking this series of questions by itself contributes to us not feeling like that anymore.

Talking to a Friend or a Mediator about Conflict

Talking to a friend or a transformative mediator about conflict which we have, is an additional tool for raising our conflict tolerance. It is important, however, that they are neutral (which mediators are trained to be) and they do not encourage us in our destructive attitude, nor try to convince us that we are wrong or advocate the other, but rather help us regain our sense of strength and responsiveness. When we talk about an issue to someone who remains neutral and tries to understand us, it helps us to distance ourselves from the issue to a certain extent, and consequently be less affected by it and at the same time to gain more clarity over the situation that we are in, and consequently a better idea on how to proceed. Seeing the situation more clearly and expanding our options and clarifying ideas on how to deal with it, is empowering in itself and helps us raise our conflict tolerance with respect to the relationship or situation in question.

Proposing Mediation or Communication Wellness

Sometimes already proposing mediation or communication wellness can do the job. When thinking of using external support for constructive or quality communication, we sometimes start thinking differently. We change our perspective and switch from adversarial to cooperative mode of thinking. And sometimes already that is enough to give us a sufficient level of conflict competence.

On the other hand, proposing mediation or communication wellness is in itself an increase in conflict tolerance, since by doing that we are not only able to correctly asses our current level of tolerance, but also, despite the level not being sufficiently high, we decide for a constructive proposal on how to proceed with the conflict in order to preserve or regain constructive interaction.

If the other side accepts our proposal, they also signal that they are in favor of a constructive outcome and as pointed out above this can switch the quality of interaction already enough to enable further constructive communication and if not, the mediator can help us with that.

Using Mediation or Communication Wellness

Obviously, raising conflict competence is a gradual process on the one hand and dealing with certain conflicts can require higher levels of conflict competence than we might possess. At the same time, it would not help if we be postponed or avoided the conflict until we are able to deal with it ourselves. Using a trained or professional mediator to help us deal with a specific conflict temporarily raises our conflict competence, since mediators and especially transformative mediators are trained to contribute to communication being constructive, i.e. they work with parties to change the interaction from negative and destructive to positive and constructive. Therefore, using the mediation or communication wellness service can contribute a great deal to compensating for our insufficient conflict competence, on the one hand, and can by helping us resolve a relatively difficult conflict contribute to raising our conflict competence, on the other.

Managing Conflict Tolerance
• Taking influences into account
• Changing the perspective
• Broader context
• Preserving or regaining internal stability
• Talking to a friend or a mediator about conflict
• Proposing mediation or communication wellness
• Using mediation or communication wellness

Table 7: Managing Conflict Tolerance

Conclusion

This book presents the concept of conflict competence as a general trait and an approach with respect to conflicts, with the intention to contribute to raising awareness and knowledge about the conflicts and to change or transform understanding, perception and consequently also dealing with conflicts in a more productive manner.

Hopefully, this book will also contribute to using the conflicts for what they can be used for, namely, development, growth and improvement of our relationships, rather than for destruction and suffering that they too often contribute to.

Using ideas and guidelines from this book individuals, couples, partners, families, groups, organizations, companies and others can gradually improve their conflict competence and contribute to more humane relationships, organizations and society. Namely, most of the people are constructive and benevolent, but fail to act accordingly when difficult conflicts emerge, since they do not understand what is happening and are not equipped nor trained to deal with conflicts constructively.

By developing better understanding, sensitivity and tolerance for conflict, we can all benefit and prosper and contribute to a more humane way of dealing with difficulties and raise the quality of our communication, relationships and life in general.

References

Bakker, C. B. & Bakker-Rabdau, M. K. (1973) No Trespassing! Explorations in Human Territoriality, Chandler & Sharp Publishers, Inc., San Francisco

Brajša, P. (1993) Pedagoška komunikologija, Glotta Nova, Ljubljana

Brandtstadter, J. & Greve, W. (1994) The ageing self: stabilizing and protective processes, *in*: Developmental Review, 14, *pp.* 52-80, Academic Press, San Diego

Bush, R.A.B. & Folger, J.P. (1994). The Promise of Mediation: Responding to Conflict Through Empowerment and Recognition, Jossey-Bass, San Francisco

Bush, R.A.B. & Folger, J.P. (2005). The Promise of Mediation: The Transformative Approach to Conflict. San Francisco: Jossey-Bass.

Čačinovič- Vogrinčič, G. (1998) Psihologija družine, Znanstveno in publicistično središče, Ljubljana

Canary, D. J. & Messman, S. J. (2000) Relationship conflict, *in*: Hendrick, C. & Hendrick, S. S.(eds.), Close relationships: A Sourcebook, Sage Publications Inc., Thousand Oaks, California

Canfield, J. & Hansen, M. V. (2001) Zgodba o Aladinu - Kako vprašati, da bi dobili, kar hočemo?, Inštitut za razvijanje osebne kakovosti, Ljubljana

Coombs, C. H. & Avrunin, G. S. (1988) The Structure of Conflict, Lawrence Erlbaum Assoc., New Jearsy

Cristopher, F. S. & Lloyd, S. A. (2000) Physical and Sexual Aggression in Relationships, *in*: Hendrick, C. & Hendrick, S. S.(eds.), Close relationships: A Sourcebook, Sage Publications Inc., Thousand Oaks, California

Fennell, M. J. V. (1989) Depression, *in*: Hawton, K., Salkovskis, P. M. & Kirk, J. (eds.), Cognitive Behaviour Therapy for Psychiatric Problems: A Practical Guide, Oxford University Press, Oxford

Filley, A. C. (1975) Interpersonal Conflict Resolution, University of Wisconsin, Madison

Forward, S. & Fraizer, D. (1998) Emotional Blackmail: When the People in Your Life Use Fear, Obligation, and Guilt to Manipulate You

Fromm, E. (1978) To Have or To Be?, Jonathan Cape, London

Fromm, E. (1997) Anatomy of Human Destructiveness, Pimlico

Glasser, W. (1985) Control Theory

Glasser, W. (2004) Warning: Psychiatry Can Be Hazardous to Your Mental Health

Goleman, D. (1995) Emotional Intelligence, Bantam Books, New York

Gordon, T. (1975) Parent Effectiveness Training, Plume

Gordon, T. (1975) Teacher Effectiveness Training, Crown

Gottman, J. M. (1994) What Predicts Divorce? The Relationship Between Marital Processes and Marital Outcomes, Lawrence Erlbaum associates, Inc., Hillsdale, New Jersey

Gray, J. (1993) What You Feel, You Can Heal: A Guide for Enriching Relationships

Heavy, C. L., Shenk, J. L. & Christensen, A. (1994) Marital conflict and divorce, *in*: L'Abate, L. (ed.) Handbook of Developmental Family Psychology and Psychopathology, John Wiley & Sons, Inc., USA

Hollander, E. P. (1981) Principles and Methods of Social Psychology, Oxford University Press, New York

Iršič, M. (2002) Guidelines and Education for a Happy Marriage, KU Leuven, Leuven, Belgium

Iršič, M. (2004) The art of Conflict Management (Umetnost obvladovanja konfliktov), Zavod Rakmo, Ljubljana

Iršič, M. (2010) Mediation (Mediacija), Zavod Rakmo, Ljubljana

Iršič, M. (2010b) Workplace Mediation (Mediacija v podjetjih), Zavod Rakmo, Ljubljana

Iršič, M. (2017) Communication Wellness, New Standards for Quality Communication in Organizations, Zavod Rakmo, Ljubljana

Iršič, M. (2018) Correlation of Conflict Tolerance and Conflict Sensitivity with Health, Work Satisfaction and Interpersonal Relationships, in: Management Challenges (Izzivi managementu), Year X, no.1, February 2018, Društvo slovenska akademija za management Ljubljana (Accepted for publication)

Johnson, C. (1993) Lucky in Love: Secrets of Happy Couples and How Their Marriages Survive

Kaplan, K. J. & O'Connor, N. A. (1993) From Mistrust to Trust: Through a Stage Vertically, *in*: Pollock, G. H. & Greenspan, S. I. (eds.) The Course of Life, Volume VI: Late Adulthood, *pp*. 173-174

Kren, A. & Iršič, M. (2015) Employees' Ability to Identify and Resolve Conflicts in Emergency Medical Service in Southeast Slovenia, Journal of Health Sciences, Faculty of Health Sciences, Novo Mesto

Kren, A. (2013) Characteristics of Conflicts in Emergency Medical Units in Southeast Slovenia, Master Thesis, University of Ljubljana

Lens, W. (1996) Motivation, *in*: De Corte, E. & Weinert, F. E. (eds.), International Encyclopedia of Developmental and Instructional Psychology, Pergamon Press, London

Lewin, K. (1948) Resolving social conflicts, Harper & Brothers, New York

Lukas Moeller, M. (1995) Resnica se začenja v dvoje, Mohorjeva družba, Celje

Mayer, R. E. (1992) Thinking, Problem Solving, Cognition (2nd edition), Freeman, New York

Miller, J. B. (1977) Toward a New Psychology of Women, Beacon Press, Boston

Pečjak, V. (1965) Poglavja iz psihologije, Državna založba Slovenije, Ljubljana

Peterson, D. R. (1983) Conflict, *in*: Kelly, H. H. (ed.), Close Relationships, W.H. Freeman and company, USA

Powell, J. & Brady, L. (1996) Will the Real Me Please Stand Up?: 25 Guidelines for Good Communication

Powell, J. (1989) Happiness is an Inside Job, Thomas Moore Publishing

Powell, J. (1995) Why Am I Afraid to Tell You Who I Am?, Thomas Moore Publishing

Raush, H. L., Barry, W. A., Hertel, R. K. (1974) Communication Conflict and Marriage, Jossey-Bass, Inc., San Francisco

Ridgewood Foundation (2002) Becoming a Third Party Neutral, Ridgewood Foundation for Community-based Conflict Resolution, Ontario, Canada

Ridgewood Foundation (2004) Foundational Process ™ Principles, Processes, Techniques and Tools, Ridgewood Foundation for Community-based Conflict Resolution, Ontario, Canada

Runde, C.E. & Flanagan, T. A. (2007) Becoming a Conflict Competent Leader, Jossey-Bass, San Francisco

Runde, C.E. & Flanagan, T. A. (2010) Developing Your Conflict Competence: A Hands-On Guide for Leaders, Managers, Facilitators, and Teams, Jossey-Bass, San Francisco

Russianoff, P. (1989) When Am I Going to Be Happy?: How to Break the Emotional Bad Habits That Make You Miserable, Bantam Books, New York

Shannon, C. & Warren, W. (1949) The Mathematical Theory of Communication, University of Illinois Press, Urbana, Illinois

Skynner, R. & Cleese, J. (1993) Families and How to Survive Them, Cedar, London

Stuart, R. B. (1982) Helping Couples Change: A Social Learning Approach to Marital Therapy, The Guilford Press, New York

Watzlawick, P. (1983) The Situation is Hopeless, But Not Serious: The Pursuit of Unhappiness, Norton, New York

Watzlawick, P., Beavin, J. H., & Jackson, D. D. (1967) The Pragmatics of Human Communication, Norton, New York

About the Author

Marko Iršič graduated in educational studies and obtained a Master's degree. He is an author, coach, mediator and trainer of mediators.

He is the author of two previous books in the Slovenian language entitled **The Art of Conflict Management** (Umetnost obvladovanja konfliktov) and **Mediation** (Mediacija) and a book entitled **Communication Wellness, New Standards for Quality Communication in Organizations**.

He founded RAKMO Institute in 2003 and it became a leading organization in transformative mediation in Slovenia. He is also a member of the board of MEDIOS – the Association of Mediation Organizations of Slovenia and president of the European Association for Transformative Mediation, as well as a member of the advisory committee of the World Forum of Mediation Centers.

His professional and voluntary work is dedicated to raising awareness about the importance of constructive conflict resolution, as well as raising the quality of communication in interpersonal relationships in general, and teaching skills and sharing knowledge that would contribute to that.

He developed the model of conflict competence in 2002 and briefly described it in the book The Art of Conflict Management (2004). Subsequently, he also developed the questionnaire presented in this book and has been using it for training courses and research purposes since then.

About Rakmo Institute

Rakmo Institute (Zavod Rakmo) was established in 2003 with the purpose of raising awareness about the importance of conflict resolution and spreading the knowledge and the skills of constructive conflict management.

Rakmo Institute is a founding member of MEDIOS – the Association of Mediation Organizations of Slovenia, a founding member of the European Association for Transformative Mediation and an active member of the World Forum of Mediation Centers.

It is at present the leading organization in the field of transformative mediation in Slovenia. Rakmo Institute also organized the 1st International Congress on Transformative Mediation in Ljubljana in 2011, the 2nd International Congress on Transformative Mediation in Ljubljana in 2014 and the 3rd International Congress on Transformative Mediation in Ljubljana in 2018.

Rakmo Institute provides training courses and seminars in transformative mediation, transformative communication, communication wellness, conflict management, anger management, stress management and in other areas of communication and personal relationships.

You can contact Rakmo Institute by writing or calling to:

Rakmo Institute – Zavod Rakmo
Parmova ul. 53, 1000 Ljubljana, Slovenia

www.rakmo.eu or www.rakmo.si/home
info@rakmo.eu or info@rakmo.si

+386 1 436 41 17

www.ingramcontent.com/pod-product-compliance
Lightning Source LLC
Chambersburg PA
CBHW071626170426
43195CB00038B/2150